D0190410

Anger

and the

Indigo Child

Anger

and the

Indigo Child

by
Dianne Lancaster

WELLNESS
PRESS

Wellness Press
Boulder, Colorado

Anger and the Indigo Child

Wellness Press / December 2002

All Rights Reserved.
Copyright © 2002 by Dianne Lancaster.
First Printing 2002.

Library of Congress Cataloging-in-Publication Data:
Lancaster, Dianne
    Anger and the Indigo Child / by Dianne Lancaster
    ISBN 0-9728904-3-2
    1. Parenting. 2. Anger. 3. Love. 4. Exceptional Children. 5. Children.
    6. Personal Growth. 7. Self-Help.

Published in the United States

For information about permission to reproduce selections
from the book, write to the address below:

Wellness Press
1750 – 30th Street, #126
Boulder, Colorado 80301
(303) 449-9922
www.emotionalwellnessinstitute.com

To Brian and Jeanne
with love

In Appreciation

♥ Val Ohanian ♥ Roy Neal ♥ Jeanne Kayser ♥ Brian Terrill ♥ Kitty Macario ♥ Jan Macario ♥ Kathleen Hammond ♥ Myra Salzer ♥ Coleen Ostlund ♥ Kay Pauley ♥ Kathleen Martin ♥ Karen Langlotz ♥ Stacy Dunevitz ♥ Melissa Michaels ♥ Robin Brody ♥ Maria Benning ♥ Ann Swenson ♥ Bea Wragee ♥ Mona Simon ♥ Char Campbell ♥ Elizabeth Gold ♥ Carl Godard ♥ Willis Thorstad ♥ Wanda Bedinghaus ♥ Teresa Sumner ♥ Richard Porter ♥ Jane Vaughan ♥ Diane Cook ♥ Barbara Barnes ♥ Holly Denise ♥ Jacquelyn Small ♥ Larry Dossey ♥ Joan Borysenko ♥ Paul, Patti and Natalie Fiske ♥ Ellen Epstein ♥ Doug Slater ♥ Channah Adler ♥ Brittany and Ashley Oldenburg ♥ 12th House Bookstore in Denver ♥ Robyn Elmslie and staff at the Veterinary Referral Center of Colorado ♥ Dark Beauty and Prince ♥

Anger and the Indigo Child

Contents

• Emotional GridLock™ • Transforming Anger Into Love™
• Emotion Modification™ • Emotional Integrity
• The Gifted/Damaged Axis™ • How Blessed We Are

• Ten of the Most Common Traits of Indigo Children
• An Indigo Child is usually an individual with
the following characteristics

• He Will Learn, But Only With Love • Where Do I Belong?
• Summer of Sams • The Anger/Power/Money/Love Axis™
• Engagable Rage™ • The Take Away's • Anger GridLock™
• The Rage/Sadness Axis™ • Love, Rage and the Possibilities
for Change • Principles for Increasing Emotional Potential
• The Needs/Capacities Axis™ • The Anger/Love Axis™
• Anger: Its Purpose and Function • Self-Health and Anger
• Understanding Anger: Avoiding Rage • Take Away's: What
Works, What Doesn't, and Why • Thank You, Sam

• 44 Ways To Show Kids You Care • Also Keep In Mind…

• An Overview of the Four Basic Emotions • I. Love: The
Enduring Emotion • Self-Love: Where It All Begins
• Love Heals • We create self-love by doing what is good for
us • We compromise self-love when we do what is not good
for us • Love and Needs • The Hierarchy of Needs • Five Ways
to Experience Love • Interpreting Our Needs • Knowing Our
Children's Needs • II. Anger: An Emotional Work-in-Progress
• The Anger You Can Trust • The Anger You Fear • III. What
We Fear and Why • Emotional Courage • Emotional Truth
• Emotional Healing • Children's Rage • Fear and Rage

To Be Nobody-But-Yourself

Almost anybody
can learn to think or believe or know,

but not a single human being
can be taught to feel.

Why?

Because whenever you think or you believe or you know,
you are a lot of other people:

but the moment you feel

you are
nobody-but-yourself.

To be nobody-but-yourself

in a world which is doing its best
night and day

to make you everybody else

means to fight the hardest battle
which any human being can fight;
and
never stop fighting.

~ e. e. cummings
October 26, 1955

From the Author

This book is in many ways my own personal story. I feel blessed and grateful to share it with you because my own life is the greatest testament I can offer as an embodiment of the principles for Transforming Anger Into Love™.

The damage I suffered in early life as a result of rage and UnLove left me hopeless and self-destructive. As an adult, my gifts in the business world were constantly sabotaged by my emotional dysfunction and instability. My relationships and marriage, my friendships and business opportunities, all were ruined by self-consuming rage, depression, manipulation, and indescribable despair.

Only when I became president of a stress management firm did I have the opportunity to work on my relationship with anger. With the support of the truly gifted individuals who blessed my life during those years, I developed this body of information that I have been teaching since 1983. Hundreds and hundreds of individuals have confirmed that these principles are life-changing, and I thank you for bringing this information into your own life at this time.

In my work with other Indigo adults, Indigo Children and their families, I am continually inspired by the gifts and potential that are often compromised by emotional dysfunction and rage. I am certain that those God-given gifts and potential have a purpose, and I feel blessed to have information that will help those individuals release their gifts and potential into the world.

As the second chapter of this book describes, I was particularly inspired by the gifted, damaged presence of three young men I met during the summer of 2002. I write about only two of them because I did not work with the third. When his mother called me, her first words were, "I'm afraid my son is going to be another Columbine headline unless we get some help." The father, a renowned scientist and extremely controlling individual, stated flatly that their home needed a new deck, and that there was not enough money for both the deck and the work the son and mother wanted to do with me.

Some day the headlines may, indeed, portray this young man's violence potential. Or, the world may instead hear of his genius in quantum physics. It is my hope that somehow this book will reach his family, and that its information will reach many families who struggle with the emotional configurations of their powerful, extraordinary Indigo Children.

My life has been blessed by many Indigo souls whose courageous application of these principles has created the pathway for readers of this book to follow. I am profoundly grateful for the presence and teaching of each of those souls. Without their powerful teaching and inspiration I would not have this information to offer. Without their devotion to the Divine Plan, I would not have experienced the meaning and purpose of my life's work. Without their powerful presence, I would not have survived the consequences of UnLove. And without their love, I would not have learned and experienced the principles of Transforming Anger Into Love™.

Thank you all.

Dianne Lancaster

Dianne Lancaster
December 27, 2002
Boulder, Colorado

Message from an Indigo Parent

My contribution to this book is in honor of the remarkable work created and activated in changing my life to an embodiment of love, through Dianne Lancaster and the principles she teaches.

I have always known since I was a child that my purpose in life was something of greatness. That knowing faded as the years went by. The lack of self-love contributed to my lost sense of self—my divine being. When my true path became a distant memory, I looked for fulfillment by fulfilling others.

For a while, I felt great joy in bringing happiness to others, without looking at how my efforts were sabotaging my journey back to the divine life plan. I turned to a darkened path—one that embodied great fear, doubt, and ultimately a lack of self-worth. I had spent so much time trying to please others that I lost complete consciousness of what I needed from the world. It was a lonely place to be by myself. To have to sit alone and think about what I needed was unthinkable and utterly unbearable.

The darkness grew deeper in my life when I married and had children. I thought, "These people depend on me. This is my life's purpose. I cannot think of my needs when my family is so in need of my presence every moment." At that point, the darkness was becoming suffocating. I was filled with anxiety and guilt, and I was starving for self-love. The denial of my needs was destroying the beautiful essence of who I was to be.

When my spiritual world began to shed some much needed light on my dismal world of darkness, I thankfully discovered that I was blessed with an Indigo Child. From the moment he was born, my son Max embraced me with a sense of love that was indescribable. Because of the immense love I had for him, I felt the best way to show him this adoration was to meet his every need, in every moment of every day that my emotional and physical capacities would allow.

During his infancy, I was miserably sleep-deprived, underweight, and over-burdened with a myriad of my unmet needs. For several years I always thought his constant neediness was just a passing phase. I was desperately trying to convince myself that more attention, more stimulating toys, or more involved activities would pacify him, even if only for moments at a time. The passing phases never came, however, and I was still plagued by frustration.

With my spiritual awakening guiding me to listen to my intuitive self, I realized that my course of action was not only producing overwhelmingly unproductive results, but that my self-confidence as a mother also was fading with the passage of time. In searching for spiritual classes and workshops that would bring me to a greater enlightenment, I gloriously embarked on a transformation toward self-love that would change my life forever and for the better.

In 2002, I was introduced, via email, to the most outstanding, exemplary tribute to self-love: Dianne Lancaster and the principles of Transforming Anger into Love™. Through several email exchanges, I learned that the immense knowledge Dianne possessed about ways to bring self-love back into my life was a relief to me greater than words would express.

At our first meeting, I knew that a major transformation was about to occur within my family.

I was also keenly aware that I would be resurrecting unloving moments, memories, and exchanges that had created these immense anger-based feelings within me. Our work was intensely gratifying, immediate, and within days, I could feel that inner child that I denied for so long, being reborn as an illuminating ray of hope and light. As the unmet needs encircling the damaged presence of my self, my husband Brad, and my children, Max and Sydney, were unveiled, it was especially important for me to microscopically look at my needs and how they could be immediately addressed.

I realized my obsessive need to clean was really a need to have someone help me with this never-ending task. It also signified that I was feverishly cleaning away my needs that I was fearful to express. I lovingly discovered that I had many extraordinary gifts that were stifled by my fear and guilt of unleashing them.

One of the needs that highlighted my entire being was the immeasurable gifts I could bring to The Anger Work™ and to this remarkable book. I knew that my contribution was the key to unlock my happiness and to expand my wings and to allow me to soar to great heights.

As I revealed my precious needs to my family, I marveled at the love beginning to emerge and overflow. I remember this heartwarming night well. One of Max's favorite stories was a book I received as a gift years ago from a prior student whom I taught in kindergarten. Inside the cover of that book, the author, Nancy Carlson, inscribed a dedication which read: "To Stacy. Follow Your Dreams."

After numerous readings of this dynamic book, *Snowden*, I held Max in my arms and said, "Max, Mommy is Snowden. Mommy has come to life." This loving tale is about a girl named Kelly, who was once taught how to ice skate, but had since forgotten. As Kelly grew older, her mother bought her a pair of used, boys' skates. Because she felt uncomfortable with the boys' skates, and with her limited abilities, Kelly self-sabotaged her attempts to skate. Giving up hope, she went to build a snowman.

When Kelly put the skates around the snowman's neck, he magically came to life. With the encouragement of the snowman's loving words and willingness to practice skating with her, Kelly's skating abilities blossomed, and so did her experience of love.

During my healing work with Dianne, I awoke in the middle of the night to realize that the magic revealed in *Snowden* was the magic Max was igniting in me. The "magic skates around my neck" was the love that was being dedicated to bring love and happiness into my life. I was watching a transformation so profound with Max that my heart ached with joy. Max and I were becoming better equipped to express our needs. His readiness was astronomically based on his outcry for me to express my needs, and for me to be released from his power in controlling me.

Part of his power was being indirectly unleashed through his eyes and the backs of his legs. For many months Max had suffered a great deal of itching with an Eczema-like rash behind his knees. We tried numerous ointments with no relief. However, as I continued to apply the information in this book, Max's legs improved remarkably. The rash was gone without a trace within a matter of days. Even though I thought I had been meeting Max's needs, I realized from reading the *Anger and the Indigo Child* manuscript that the rash was his unexpressed anger and feelings of vulnerability.

As my transformation experience became more intense, Max's right eye became so red and encrusted with pus that it resembled Pink Eye. Through working with Dianne, I came to understand that the condition in his eye was unexpressed sadness... because I was not expressing my needs. After I intensely addressed my anger issues for a couple of days, the clear, radiant, crystal blue of Max's eyes returned, leaving his doctors in complete disbelief.

I now realize the remarkable gifts that young Indigo Children possess. They are here to guide us if we take their hand, to teach us if we listen, to show us who we can be if we release the locks and chains, and to love us if we open our hearts.

My deepest love and gratitude for this spiritual expedition go to my family, my friends, and my divine guides who have encouraged me to pursue my dreams of shining with an immense amount of love and soulful purpose.

For you, my dear friends and readers, let this book help you find the love within yourself, the compassion for the journey ahead, and the many blessings of guidance in fulfilling your greatest soul potential. Because we are on our own but we are not alone, you, too, can experience the joy of Transforming Anger Into Love™.

To those who have assisted me in this process, I dedicate this message with immeasurable love, for: Dianne Lancaster, the healing presence of Prince, and for Jeanne Kayser, Karen Langlotz, Roy Neal, Bea Wragee, Val Ohanian, Wanda Bedinghaus, M.D., Joe Nicols, the Sumner family, the Miller family, and the Gaither family... for their time, devotion and above all else, LOVE.

This soulful journey could not have been possible without the love and spiritual guidance from my parents, Marilyn and Jerry Jacobs.

Stacy Diane Dunevitz
Indigo Parent

Introduction

In an ideal world, the supply of love within and around us would be adequate to meet our needs. Then anger would not be necessary. For now, however, in some families, some of the time, anger is indeed an issue. The principles of Transforming Anger Into Love™ can help.

Although this book is about anger, its purpose is to increase our relationship with love. Anger is the principal emotion that blocks our connection to love. These principles will help you understand and redirect the anger you and your children are experiencing so that you all can experience more love. This book is directed to the Indigo Children and families because working with them has been such an inspiration to me. However, these principles are helpful to every child, every family, and every person who is seeking emotional wellness.

Toward the end of writing this book, I was talking with Bea Wragee. She works closely with Nancy Tappe, who first announced to the world that the Indigo Children had arrived. Bea is also the parent of an Indigo Child. In the second Indigo book by authors Lee Carroll and Jan Tober, *An Indigo Celebration*, an exchange between Bea and her son had gotten my attention.

"Why are you so angry, Mommy?" the exchange began and then depicted a mother's typical, "I'm not mad," automatic response. When her child asked, "Then why do you have that mad look on your face?" Bea acknowledges in the book, "The truth was the truth! I was angry, and his sensitivity to my body language and expressions was accurate. Now could I be enough of an adult to admit it? Would I discount his reality or honor his awareness?

"Mustering some courage, I told him, 'You're right, honey, I am angry about something that happened today, and I didn't tell you the truth. I apologize.'

"My son's gift to me that day was awareness of being my *whole self*, and to be honest about things. How can you teach a child to tell the truth if you're unable to do it yourself?"

In our conversation, Bea was commenting on the title of this book, *Anger and the Indigo Child*. She said, "It's not the Indigo Children who have the anger problem. It's the rest of us whose anger gets triggered by them." The book, Bea suggested, would be better directed to us rather than them.

As the gods would have it, Bea's observation matched the final inspiration that came to me after the September 28, 2002, Anger and the Indigo Child workshop. The parents and teachers who attended confirmed what I had encountered in so many individual and family settings: many parents and teachers do not understand some of the emotional configurations and needs of these powerful young Beings. In addition, many parents are passing on the discipline model they grew up with. The results fit the term I use for the consequences of entangled anger-based patterns: Emotional GridLock™.[1]

Emotional GridLock™

The anger grids are troubling and painful for any child and family. But they are more so for Indigo Children and families, for two important reasons.

1. These children know that their extraordinary gifts and potential are at risk if their emotional integration and development do not complement their gifts and potential; and

---

[1] This and other terms are explained in the Glossary section.

2. The Indigo Children are here to help us elders learn emotional options and strategies for working with these children so that we, too, can evolve our own emotional adequacy and competency.

And thank goodness. Surely no one active enough to have found this book can deny the buildup of anger, abuse, violence, and rage across the planet. The medical, educational, faith-based, and mental health disciplines are not adequately addressing this emotional dysfunction. Therefore, the question in my mind has been, how *are* we going to stem this epidemic? How many Columbines, workplace shootings, and headlines of unconscionable acts of child and spousal abuse will it take? For those who *are* willing to take a look at their own anger and emotional dysfunction, what is in place for them? Is it easy to find help with anger in the Yellow Pages? Is there a 1-800-Anger911 24-hour helpline? Are there storefronts in local strip malls shouting, "Need Help With Anger? Stop In."?

Despite a $12 billion industry in anti-depressants, are people really more emotionally healthy? Or is it possible they have simply gone from *de*pressed to *sup*pressed, by way of "a jagged little pill"?

Transforming Anger Into Love™

Doing The Anger Work™ (as I refer to this body of information) since 1980, I have developed my own conclusions. I also have developed some principles for addressing the anger, both individually and collectively. These principles are taught in the training and certification program outlined in Chapter Sixteen. They also are reflected throughout this book in the various guidelines for Transforming Anger Into Love™.

The principles have been taught and refined in a variety of settings: for individuals, families, schools, businesses, professional organizations, sports organizations, prisons, and faith-based institutions. The principles are presented here not only *to* the Indigo Children, but also *for* them. The recent workshops, together with my 19 years of working with Indigo Children and families, have confirmed that the elders can help the children most when their own anger is also addressed. As my associate Jeanne Kayser has insisted every day since we met, most people do not understand anger. The Anger Work™ is, therefore, principally an *educational* challenge.

"People do not know what to do with anger," Jeanne has said so many times. "They do not know how to change their own patterns. Given the stigma attached to anger from our generation's past conditioning, there is also still an inclination to deny or judge or feel shame about anger."

It is certainly time for change in that regard, and the Indigo Children are part of that "grand plan." This book is, therefore, about change. In the chapter titled *Anger, Rage and the Possibilities for Change* (a map someone once characterized as "from hell-ness to well-ness,"), certain of the principles for understanding and managing anger are outlined.

In *Conditions of Emotional Dysfunction*, the step-by-step development of anger into rage is detailed. And the chapter titled *Return to Love* offers specific Rage Reversal™ how-to's.

One of the main anger-related challenges for us as elders in Indigo Children's lives is to recognize that our competency and curriculum for applying these principles in behalf of the children lies in our own personal application and expertise. Accordingly, much of this book is written for the elders, so that we can co-create with our children an environment for emotional health and healing. Throughout the years, I have consistently encountered dedicated, well-meaning parents and teachers whose anger-based patterns fused with the children's in seemingly intractable ways.

In my workshops and teaching, therefore, I have learned to help the elders identify the anger-based patterns they may be perpetuating, and to teach them how to dismantle those patterns in their own behalf. Only then can they help the children recognize and reverse those patterns in *their* lives.

Sometimes this is not what elders want to hear. I particularly recall that experience at a state conference for foster care and adoption parents and personnel. My workshops were the first to sell out at that conference, given the titles "Managing the Angry Child" and "Understanding and Managing Anger." Many of those parents were woefully unequipped to handle the emotional challenges of the children they were trying to help. Some parents' anger even came out in the course of the workshops. Just recounting how the children "push my buttons" would send them into unmanaged emotional angst.

"We want to know what to do about *them*," was the generic message in the room. "We just need to know some techniques and some (more) behavior modification tools. We don't want to look at this as an *emotional* issue. We feel more powerful and secure if we can deal with their *acting-out* behaviors."

I only wish it could be so.

Emotion Modification™

Uncontrolled anger is an *emotional* challenge. It requires, I will suggest, Emotion Modification™ techniques as well as behavior modification. In this book's second chapter about a particularly tormented young man, you will see that despite his extreme destructive tendencies, the anger management techniques suggested for him included hitting his mattress with a soft bat. I am convinced that hitting *anything* to defuse rage is like re-arranging the deck chairs on the Titanic. It's what we suggest when we don't know anything else to do.

This book is therefore filled with how-to's. *44 Ways to Show Kids You Care*, how to identify *Hidden Symptoms of Anger*™, how to utilize the *Hidden Power of Love*, and how to interpret the *Symbology* of suppressed anger stored in organs and systems in the body. In addition, there are journaling exercises for parents, teachers and kids. Needs inventories for parents, teachers and kids. How-to's, don't do's, why to's… not only for the children, but also for ourselves.

This book is in many ways an educational tool. It dissects the anger-based patterns and grids that form and lock people into automatic unproductive behaviors and outcomes. It teaches the *Conditions of Emotional Dysfunction*: how the conditions of depression, anxiety, dependency, and withdrawal develop. And in perhaps the most helpful portions of the book, the principles for reversing rage are set forth. In those sections you will find that while love is the emotion that manages anger, sadness is the key to reversing rage.

Emotional Integrity

The Anger Work™ is a work-in-progress. Much is yet to be learned. Even more is yet to be applied. If you look through this book for the 1, 2, 3's for making the children's behavior easier to live with, you will find the foundation for the success of those steps enhanced by your own increased emotional integrity and power.

Integrity is of huge importance to Indigo Children. They have astounding intuitive capacities and can spot a lie or deceit the instant we even think about it. When we opt for those kinds of powerless responses to their very powerful Beings, they lose respect for us immediately. Being truthful with someone is the greatest honor we can offer anyway; and with these children, it is imperative. Doing otherwise engages their anger. Being so continually engages their rage.

As this book's chapter on Ritalin and emotional integrity boldly states, Indigo Children possess a high level of emotional intelligence, and they regret and resent when we, the elders, model something lesser. They know they must learn from us. They also know we must learn from them. In the Principles of *Transforming Anger Into Love*™, the success of positive emotional change is contingent on a single capacity: the enduring presence of love.

Love is indeed the emotion that manages anger. It is the emotion that gives us options to anger—like patience, understanding, compassion, and forgiveness. So long as our anger is loving, it is safe. Our children may not like our anger, but they can trust it if it is accompanied with love. If we are in touch with love for ourselves and for our children as we express our anger, then what we are saying and we are doing as we express the anger tells *us* our anger is safe and trustworthy.

Anyone who is surprised to hear that anger and love are designed to co-exist will be encouraged to read *Anger, Rage and the Possibilities for Change*. Those principles state that anger is a God-given emotion. It has a purpose. And whereas anger is a more intense emotion than love, love is more enduring. Anger is purposefully designed to be a non-enduring emotion. It is such an unpleasant and uncomfortable emotion, we ideally want to release it from ourselves as soon as possible.

As an ordinary, even appropriate response to certain daily-life events, anger (as contrasted with rage) has proportionality. It has integrity. It loses both, however, when it is manipulated and suppressed. When that occurs, the anger-based patterns that develop accumulate into the uncontrolled, uncontrollable, destructive condition of rage. I have worked with many families whose Indigo Children's gifts and potential were at risk because of rage. As this book outlines, even those conditions can often be transformed.

The Gifted/Damaged Axis™

Some people insist categorically that Indigo Children are wisps of spiritual lightness, gentleness, and love. That is certainly true of some Indigo Children. I have had the honor to know such children. One of them is Jan, the first Indigo Child I write about in this book. He is not, however, typical of the many, many other Indigo Children whose anger and self-contempt I have encountered over the years. Those children I rank along the Gifted/Damaged Axis™ because it seems that their exceptional gifts and potential are almost equally matched with consuming self- and other-destruction.

The young man named Sam in this book is one of those whose situation was soul searing for me. The abject emotional bleakness of his so-called-life spoke to me deeply. To try anything other than punishment and control with Sam was out of the question for the caregivers who asked me to help with his anger. In far too many families, either controlling or drugging the Indigo Children is their approach. As this book suggests, however, there are many other alternatives.

Indigo Children's emotional needs and presence certainly can be powerful. Those needs and presence can be behaviorally challenging. When our own emotional needs are met and our own emotional presence is powerful, we are able to model and create the options our children need. For that reason, certain information in this book is dedicated to enhancing the elders' emotional power and presence.

How Blessed We Are

Alongside many Indigo Children there are many devoted, powerful, caring parents and teachers, guardians and mentors, family members and friends. Their presence is a gift and inspiration. Their courage produces powerful breakthroughs and healing. In many instances, these individuals have contributed to my own insights and learning. I am therefore thankful for each teacher, each lesson, each child and family whose stories are either woven or remembered in this book.

The information in this book is far from everything we need to know. Nor does it represent everything I have to teach. It is, however, a start. It is a way to begin to reach the children, families, and others with insights into the patterns and conditions that can limit all of us in our emotional growth and potential.

These are interesting times on Planet Earth. The changes so many of us talked about and prepared for have come in ways we could never have anticipated. Once again, we bow to the infinite wisdom and unfolding of the Divine Plan.

I have said for decades that there is, indeed, a plan for evolving the anger on the planet. I also wondered for decades how that could possibly be, when what I saw was the cumulative dysfunction spreading further and deeper into the collective's psyche and soul. The Indigo Children are surely urging us toward a new emotional mandate. We are to be love, we are to be loving, and we are to Be in accordance with our highest purpose and potential. This is what Indigo Children inspire. It is what they expect. It is what they teach. And it is what they need.

How blessed we are.

How To Benefit from This Book

By Jeanne Kayser

When I was introduced to the principles of Transforming Anger Into Love™, my first reaction was, "How logical these principles are," and, "Why haven't I heard this information before?" I've now come to the conclusion that the child-rearing and emotional models my parents had, and their generations before them, had just been automatically passed down from one generation to the next. No one had questioned the relevancy or applicability of that information, and the reason nothing had changed through all those generations was, possibly, because no one had any better answers to offer.

Parents, children, and teachers in the Anger and the Indigo Child workshops have responded in the same way. "This makes perfect sense," they have said with amazement as they heard these principles for understanding and managing anger. Then the group would discuss and confirm how the information that we all had received from our parents was totally inadequate and often inappropriate for the challenges we face with our children today.

Because the principles in this book are new to most of us, I find it helpful to have them reinforced throughout the book and presented in a variety of different contexts. To be most beneficial, this book is presented with two reading styles in mind: for those readers who like to read from the front cover completely through to the back cover; and for those readers who are particularly interested in certain subjects and will go directly to those first. Each chapter therefore builds on the principles of Transforming Anger Into Love™.

Even if you are typically a "subject" reader, I certainly recommend that you read this entire book. It is an invaluable reference guide for how-to information, how-to exercises, and for sheer inspiration. There is new and valuable information in every chapter. While each chapter contains its own set of applicable principles, no matter how many times I've read them, I always discover something that had escaped my attention earlier.

Since I have been applying the principles in this book, I have experienced tremendous changes in the way I approach life, the way I understand life, the choices I make in my life, and my continuing ability to create more love in my life. These are options I never had imagined were possible. I know your own options and inspiration will expand, too, as you apply the principles for Transforming Anger Into Love™.

Chapter One

Indigo Indicators

Indigo Children are extraordinary, gifted, wonderful Beings. The three Indigo books (cited in Chapter Two) preceding this one are essential reading for anyone seeking to know more about these children. For readers who are not familiar with Indigo Children, the following are descriptions offered by the principal authors on this topic:

From Lee Carroll and Jan Tober
Co-Authors, *The Indigo Children*.

Ten of the Most Common Traits of Indigo Children[1]

1. They come into the world with a feeling of royalty (and often act like it).
2. They have a feeling of "deserving to be here," and are surprised when others don't share that.
3. Self-worth is not a big issue. They often tell the parents "who they are."
4. They have difficulty with absolute authority (authority without

---

[1] Throughout this book, numbered references not footnoted are explained in the Quoted Material section, page 231.

explanation or choice).

5. They simply will not do certain things; for example, waiting in line is difficult for them.

6. They get frustrated with systems that are ritual-oriented and don't require creative thought.

7. They often see better ways of doing things, both at home and in school, which makes them seem like "system busters" (nonconforming to any system).

8. They seem antisocial unless they are with their own kind. If there are no others of like consciousness around them, they often turn inward, feeling like no other human understands them. School is often extremely difficult for them socially.

9. They will not respond to "guilt" discipline ("Wait till your father gets home and finds out what you did.").

10. They are not shy in letting you know what they need.

From Doreen Virtue, Ph.D.
Author, *The Care and Feeding of Indigo Children*.

An Indigo Child is usually an individual with the following characteristics:[2]

1. Strong-willed
2. Born in 1978 or later
3. Headstrong
4. Creative, with an artistic flair for music, jewelry making, poetry, etc.
5. Prone to addictions
6. An "old soul," as if they're 13, going on 43
7. Intuitive or psychic, possibly with a history of seeing angels or deceased people
8. An isolationist, either through aggressive acting-out, or through fragile introversion
9. Independent and proud, even if they're constantly asking you for money
10. Possesses a deep desire to help the world in a big way
11. Wavers between low self-esteem and grandiosity

12. Bores easily
13. Has probably been diagnosed as having ADD or ADHD
14. Prone to insomnia, restless sleep, nightmares, or difficulty/fear of falling asleep
15. Has history of depression or even suicidal thoughts or attempts
16. Looks for real, deep, and lasting friendships
17. Easily bonds with plants or animals

Continued from Doreen Virtue:

- "…Indigos are as varied as there are shades of the color blue. We *need* variety among Indigos. Yet, if your children responded positively to 14 or more of the above characteristics, then they're most likely Indigos. If they related to between 11 and 13 of the above characteristics, they're probably 'Indigos in training,' or those who are just developing their… traits. These descriptions could also apply to Indigo Children who are being artificially detached from their spiritual gifts, through the use of authoritative force and/or Ritalin.[2]
- "We know that Indigo Children are born wearing their God-given gifts on their sleeves. Many of them are natural-born philosophers who think about the meaning of life and how to save the planet. They are inherently gifted scientists, inventors, and artists.
- "Many gifted children are mistakenly thought to be 'learning disabled,' according to the National Foundation for Gifted and Creative Children. …According to the leaders of this organization, 'Many gifted children are being destroyed in the public education system. Many gifted children are being falsely labeled with ADHD. And many parents are unaware that their child could be potentially gifted.'

"They [the Foundation] list the following characteristics to help you identify whether your child is **gifted**:
- Has high sensitivity.
- Has excessive amounts of energy.
- Bores easily—may appear to have a short attention span.
- Requires emotionally stable and secure adults around him/her.

- Will resist authority if it's not democratically oriented.
- Has preferred ways of learning, particularly in reading and math.
- May become easily frustrated because they have big ideas but lack the resources or people to assist them in carrying these tasks to fruition.
- Learns from an exploratory level, resisting rote memory or just being a listener.
- Cannot sit still unless absorbed in something of their own interest.
- Is very compassionate; has many fears such as death and loss of loved ones.
- If they experience failure early, may give up and develop permanent learning blocks.[1]
- "If you're an adult who relates to the above characteristics, it's possible that you were one of the first forerunners of the Indigo Children."[2]

From Nancy Tappe
Author, *Understanding Your Life Through Color*.

The first person to identify and write about the Indigo phenomenon in her 1986 book, Nancy Tappe says of Indigo Children:

"They believe in themselves."[1]

Chapter Two

The Gift of Their Presence
and The Presence of Their Gifts

He Will Learn, But Only With Love

The first Indigo Child I knew was in 1983. I was president of a stress management firm and teaching the principles of Transforming Anger Into Love™ in workshops and one-on-one sessions with our clients. Our firm ordered Louise Hay's little blue book, *Heal Your Body*, by the dozens in those days, handing them out at workshops and to each new client. As pioneers in understanding the symbology of energy stored in the body, we were thrilled to find someone else exploring these realms.

One of our clients who was especially spiritual talked often about her 3-year old grandson whom she referred to as "this special Being."

"The first time I held him and looked into his eyes, I knew he was an ancient soul," Kitty would say matter of factly. And indeed, as she continued to share with me the challenges this young Being presented to their family's traditional approach to parenting and disciplining, it became clear this child was exceptional—as was his grandmother.

"We have such wonderful conversations," she would say when Jan was in grade school, "but he's so young to be asking such profound questions!" Still, the awe and delight were obvious as she recounted Jan's questions about the universe and its plan for all beings, creatures, molecules, and such. With a twinkle in her eye, and half-way feigning exasperation, Kitty would say, "He wants to know *everything*, and all I can do is tell him what I know, and encourage him to keep asking."

Over the years, Kitty advocated fiercely for her grandson. "Just let him Be!" she must have said a thousand times. "He knows who he is. He knows what he needs. Just listen to him. Trust him. Let him tell us how to help him prepare for life."

"But he needs to learn responsibility!" both the father and grandfather would insist. "He'll never get through life drawing and doing art!" Because Kitty knew Jan's spiritual side intimately, however, she knew art was only one of his gifts. She trusted that with such gifts, Jan would find his purpose and career.

"The others in the family didn't understand where he was coming from, and would criticize him when he did something that was different from their way," Kitty said recently when recounting her memories for this book. "The males—grandfathers and uncles in the family, especially—would want to correct him and tell him there was a better, easier way. It was a very difficult situation.

"I would just keep saying to all of them, 'He's a free soul. Don't be authoritative. Don't force him to do things your way! Treat him gently. He will learn, but only with love.'"

Where Do I Belong?

Almost 20 years later, now that I know the term and general characteristics, I recognize how many Indigo Children and families I've worked with across the country—and how blessed Jan's life has been in comparison to so many. "Scholar of the Year" in the philosophy department from which he graduated Summa Cum Laude. No problems adapting to public middle school. No uncontrolled anger. Employed now by an agency that helps children and families. "To this day, he reaches out to perfect strangers, and within seconds, he's talking with them as though he has known them forever," his grandmother says, confirming what Nancy Tappe says of the Humanist Indigos in her interview with Jan Tober: "They'll talk to anyone, anytime—friendly, friendly, friendly."[1]

As I contrast Jan's upbringing and outcome to the three young men I encountered in the summer of 2002, I come to the essence of why I'm writing this book at this time. It is inspired by the emotional challenges of the children who have candidly said:

- "I don't feel like I belong here."
- "I don't relate to my family."
- "No one understands me."
- "I just stay angry."

Thankfully, such identity issues have been written about in *The Indigo Children*, the seminal book on Indigo Children by Lee Carroll and Jan Tober; in *The Care and Feeding of Indigo Children* by Doreen Virtue, Ph.D.; and later in *The Indigo Celebration*, the Carroll and Tober follow-up book. Offering profound insights and information from a wide variety of parents, professionals, and Indigo Children, these groundbreaking books finally enlightened the world that indeed, these children have arrived! And they have brought with them some new and unique challenges.

Consider, for example, this spectrum of characteristics that usually apply to these children:

- Sensitive
- Gifted
- Creative
- Emotional outbursts
- Feel and act like royalty
- Strong willed
- Bored easily
- Behavior problems
- Do not respond to traditional discipline techniques
- Isolationist behaviors through aggressive acting-out or fragile introversion
- Authority issues
- History of depression, suicidal thoughts or attempts
- Often Labeled ADD/ADHD
- Significant fears: for example, of being in shopping malls, of the weather, and of falling asleep
- They believe in themselves

Their parents and teachers usually believe in these children, too. Astounded by the children's gifted intellect and insights, adults in their lives often scramble to respond adequately and productively… not only to these children's minds, but also to their emotional power, to their emotional intelligence, and to their intense emotional needs.

That is when I meet them.

Summer of Sams

"It's the volatility I can't handle," a teacher, her voice cracking, said to me on the phone. "It's ruining everything, at home *and* at school. He's thrown his stereo through the wall, kicked in doors, and cut his arms with knives. Since his sister tells the kids at school what he does, they keep their distance. They're a little afraid."

With that, my summer of meeting three young men with similar names and similar situations began. For purposes of this book, they will be called "Sam."

"You will love him," this teacher went on to assure me in this, our first conversation. "You will instantly see why I am devoting so much energy to his situation. He is so bright. So gifted. So intuitive and charming, you will wonder if indeed this is the same soul who tried to kill his father."

Given my startle response to the surprising end of that sentence, I took note. Aside from the work I had done in the prison system, I couldn't recall knowingly working with anyone so potentially threatening. And I wasn't sure I wanted to. When the teacher told me more about Sam's background, however, I felt inclined at least to meet him.

As this teacher described Sam's behavior, it was clear that his anger had turned into rage. While the distinction between anger and rage is fully outlined in the *Transforming Anger Into Love*™ chapter, for now I will say simply that when anger is suppressed and stored up inside, it eventually loses proportionality and becomes uncontrollable. That is when the creative properties of anger turn into the destructive properties of rage. Rage is an extreme condition. For Sam's rage to have reached the point of such self-destructive behavior that he had cut himself, thrown and broken things on a regular basis, and threatened to kill his father, it was clear to me that his experience of UnLove[1] was extreme.

I use the term UnLove specifically because children can be in the

---

[1] This and other terms are explained in the Glossary section.

presence of love, but not necessarily be *experiencing* that love. Since love is humanity's most significant emotional need, it is understandable to me that a child who has lived without adequate love may manipulate, destroy, and act out as an expression of needing love. On the other hand, my experience with many Indigo Children is that when they experience authenticity in another person, their manipulations and self-destructive actions often dissolve. I therefore looked forward to meeting Sam's guardians. Then I could begin to identify the patterns of power and control that are always factors in anger/rage conditions. Those patterns are also the primary source for dismantling those conditions.

Having elected not to press charges for attempted murder, Sam's parents had arranged for "one last chance" to see if he could "turn out to be something other than a menace to society." That chance came through a counselor and educator couple who had close ties to the family. Aware of the details of Sam's situation, they had agreed to the legal guardian role, with the stipulation that a multidisciplinary team of their associates also would be retained by the family as additional overseers and advisors in this situation.

The group was convinced that this particular elite private school Sam was attending would "work wonders" for him. At school, Sam's teacher told me, that had indeed occurred. He was thriving academically. A gifted orator and writer, he acted in and directed his own theater productions throughout the metropolitan area. For this he gained acknowledgment and respect from teachers and students alike. Off stage, however, his "performance" was dismal. While he said it was by his own choosing that he had no friends at this large-for-a-private-school setting, the sadness in his eyes as he said "no friends" said otherwise.

There were many adults in Sam's life, however, and not just from the team of elders brought in by his parents. Sam was the type of person adults enjoyed being with. After meeting him, I understood why. He seemed to know something about everything—sports teams, vintage movies, history, art, philosophy, grunge music, classical music, politics, and technology especially. He was informed, engaging, and yes, he could be quite charming. But not with schoolmates. It was the team's consensus that if Sam's alienation from his peers could be resolved, that would create the platform needed for his social integration. In turn, they surmised,

Sam's troublesome emotional patterns would improve, and this strategy would eventually contribute to the outcome everyone was seeking: peace, well-being, and actualization of his gifts and potential.

"He is making progress in his new home," these elders assured me frequently. Then, tentatively, they would add some type of qualifier along the lines of, "There is just some emotional guidance he's not getting... for his anger."

In the several times I met with the team before meeting Sam, almost inevitably someone in the group would recite the ways Sam had acted out, and what they had taken away or restricted as a result. They were convinced that this reductionist method that gave them more power and security was also teaching Sam some necessary social traits. They wanted to know how to create even more structure for Sam emotionally so that his violent outbursts would decrease.

The Anger/Power/Money/Love Axis™

"We also want him to learn responsibility with money," the guardians tagged on to the agenda for my work with him. "For every day he doesn't hit or throw, he gets one dollar added to his allowance. If he does hit or throw, we take away two dollars for each incident." Not wanting to even ask what the balance in his account or the history of its fluctuations was, I simply explained that in The Anger Work™, I suggest not using money as an incentive or punishment.

"But why?" three of the team members asked incredulously. I started by recapping the obvious. Sam was an extraordinary young man in many ways. His gifts and potential were profound. He knew he was different, even special. He and the team had talked about how his interests were so varied, and how his wide-ranging capabilities were so exceptional. The elders were, they acknowledged, awestruck by Sam's intellect and wisdom. "He talks about the world like a statesman," a team member had remarked. In some ways, I explained, those very qualities accounted for what his guardians labeled as "arrogance."

It was confusing for this team of elders to witness Sam fluctuate from acting "arrogant" one day, to feeling worthless and hopeless the next. Not having encountered the Indigo books yet, I couldn't quote Carroll and Tober's passage of, "They come into the world with a feeling of royalty (and often act like it),"[1] but for several years I had used the term Gifted/Damaged. The team could relate to that axis in Sam. It was a challenge for me, however, to explain how that axis requires careful consideration when combining money, value, and self-worth.

I began by suggesting to Sam's team what I had said to numerous families before. "Everyone here is struggling to find ways to reduce Sam's destructive behavior. He gets angry, the guardians get angry, the teachers get angry… there is clearly a lot of anger to work with. Yet, love is the emotion that manages anger. Love is also the emotion that sustains positive change. If the money agreements have been made with love, are being enforced with love, and are being enforced consistently, then they are likely to work. Then they will not confuse the issue of self-value and self-worth. But I often encounter situations where the adults use money because they have run out of emotional options. They use it as an effort to control. Sometimes even to bribe and coerce.

"Until the automatic anger patterns are worked out in this situation," I said directly to the guardians, whose role was to convey the money to Sam, "it is my suggestion not to combine money with the power struggles already in place. For example, let's say that Sam 'earns' the money when he is 'good.' Everyone is no doubt glad that he has complied with the rules. But what if, when it is time for you to give him the money he has earned, he has done something outside the rules. You give him the money, but in anger. These dynamics fuse money and power with anger and love. Your emotional patterns and fluctuations, and the ways you use money, can create an inconsistent message to Sam about his value and self-worth.

"The result of that combination of values and messages can be very complex. My suggestion is that we make progress on dismantling the anger patterns, and then make new agreements about Sam and money and rewards for following the rules."

After that, it was time for my first meeting with Sam.

Engagable Rage™

At our original meeting, I recognized the internal inferno inside Sam, despite his obvious efforts to cover it. Although it was activated less often these days, the rage was there, doing what rage does: taking all the suppressed anger he dared not express for fear of more punishment, alienation, and "take away's," and exiling that once-purposeful anger into a cumulative reservoir from whence it would eventually make its way to the surface.

I didn't want to characterize what could happen if Sam didn't get some relief soon. I didn't want to take away from the fact that his volatility was less frequent and threatening than it had been. But when a person has a history of rage and no intervention has been directed at the emotional patterns connected to it, Engagable Rage™ is a constant threat. The person may be able to control the rage temporarily; but lurking underneath that effort is a condition of extreme emotional dysfunction. It is the result of someone's emotional options being so completely stripped away—or perhaps so undeveloped—that the reservoir of manipulated anger builds beyond the person's capacity to control it. The person whose rage had gone quiet for a while blasts forth from zero to 100.

These patterns are so well developed and powerful that they are, indeed, uncontrollable. The energy fueling them is neither disbursed with conscious thought or intent, nor is that energy controllable with conscious thought or intent. Rage is an emotional condition. It is the long-term buildup of long-term unmet needs for love. It is an anguished scream for love. Rage must, therefore, be dismantled and redirected through Emotion Modification™.

Sam's counselors had hoped the recently implemented anger management techniques would help him control his rage. The techniques included hitting a pillow, wringing a towel, and hitting his mattress with a soft bat when his anger got out of control. Sam snickered when I asked if this had helped. His, 'If it had worked we wouldn't be here today,' look said a lot. "Did you try the techniques?" I asked.

"I've tried everything everyone has suggested," he said, "and nothing lasts."

Admitting they had derived no sustainable change from the towel wringing and other techniques, a team member wondered aloud one day why Sam continued to be uncontrollable even though he had these safe ways of discharging his anger. I offered at least one explanation. "These types of physical activities can help to discharge some of the pressure of emotions that gather in the body and build to the point of rage. However, without adequate attention to the emotional patterns that fuel the rage, only its frequency will be modified. Not its potential."

The team had also sent Sam to meditation classes. "He flunked," one team member said with combined sarcasm and disbelief. They had tried massage and weight lifting, too, to help reduce the rage potential. For now, they had collectively rejected drug intervention, so their principal approach to Sam resembled what other families often do when they run out of emotional options. They tried control, discipline, and behavior modification techniques passed down over time and (I suggest gingerly, here), not sufficiently updated to address the emotional configurations and needs of the Indigo Children I have worked with.

The Take Away's

Shortly before I arrived on the scene, Sam had put 13 miles more on his car's odometer than the mileage to and from his fast-food job. His guardians checked the mileage each time he left home and logged it as soon as he returned. That, they said, is how they knew he went somewhere without permission. Although Sam had an explanation, the issues of trust in this situation were fraying fast.

Sam's guardians' answer to this demonstration of Sam's "continually not being trustworthy" was to take away the car. "He can ride his bike to school and work," they had concluded. "He's strong and fit," was the rationale they used. They also were rapidly using up their "take away" options. Of necessity, they had to hold onto the hope that one of these tactics was going to work, and that they would ultimately "win." They had tried everything else, they said. "Taking away things that matter is the only strategy that works."

From what I could determine, what "worked" for them was that Sam relinquished privileges and possessions without becoming enraged at that take-away moment. He complied, and that was good because it meant he was learning to control his rage. The risk from his rage internalizing, into depression, for example, was not the immediate focus or concern. This group was looking for behavior changes. This take-away strategy was lessening his acting out, so it was working for them.

For them to finally "win" seemed to mean that Sam would have been stripped of so much that he finally would comply with all their rules. He would make good grades, get along with classmates, arrive at work on time, save his money, not eat in his room, keep the volume of his music down, wash and fold his own clothes, help clean the house on weekends, spend only short amounts of time on the phone (when it was returned to him, that is), and not rent unacceptable videos like "Welcome to the Doll House."

"It's about a depressed teenager. Sam is depressed enough. That film just reinforces his low self-esteem." These were the comments from the team who had never seen the video, and had never talked with Sam about why he had rented it about 30 times. They had only heard from other families that it was not a good influence, and they were definitely trying to be a good influence on Sam.

That influence mostly took the form of introducing and emphasizing rules for being accountable, responsible, considerate, and well behaved. If Sam did not demonstrate that he was learning to increase those behaviors, the team saw their role as imposing appropriate consequences. The option of *adding* something to Sam's enjoyment of life—or, especially, giving back anything that had been taken away—was in many ways inconceivable to this team. They were convinced that Sam had to learn from this way of teaching and conditioning. This situation was, as a result, a prime example of Anger GridLock™ in play.

Anger GridLock™

The team members, particularly the guardians, became angry when Sam did not comply with the rules and boundaries they had established. They used their anger in an effort to convince or force Sam to comply. When that did not work, they manipulated privileges and objects, hoping those had sufficient meaning to him that he would change his behavior in order to have them.

Having used up most of his anger options, Sam's only remaining response was rage, which he was trying hard to restrain. He did, however, manage to utilize its destructive properties by temporarily destroying inside himself whatever meaning the privileges and possessions previously had.

Whatever the team did, Sam matched. Whatever he did, they did more. Somewhere in this grid, each side would have to yield. That was the only way the entrenched anger-based patterns could be reworked. The patterns had locked each side into automatic, unloving responses. During times when the guardians were spewing, "You're not going to be able to do this," and "You're not going to be able to do that," their own anger was out of control. Sam knew this and resented it. He needed to experience emotional power greater than his own power to drive people to the edge. More than that, Sam needed to experience emotional power that was *loving* and greater than his own.

Sam also needed to regain some sense of why the hard work to gain dominion over his emotional outbursts was even worth it. He needed an experience of love, including self-love, really soon. The team needed to feel a sense of hope, as well. More than once, in conversations about what they had taken away or threatened to do if his behavior did not change, Sam had looked downward, slowly shaking his head. He seemed to say, "This is not the answer. More of what we are already doing is not the answer. I need something else, and so do they."

The team did not exactly admit to contemplating a worst-case scenario, but they did once talk about what if they reached a point where there was nothing else to do (*i.e.*, nothing else to take away), and Sam was still uncontrollable. To continue feeling that they were contributing positively to this situation, they had to eventually feel the power and relief of having some options other than to reduce and control. Those options and feelings of relief would have to occur on the emotional level. For a while, though, I wasn't certain what else to try in order to steward the focus from behavior-based change to emotion-based change. More than once I had tried reminding them of my comments about sadness when we first met. "You described him perfectly before even meeting him," the team had already acknowledged. But it was the sadness underneath the rage that I had described, and the desperation of such extreme emotional alienation, and fear, and need.

At that meeting, before I had met Sam, tears had welled up inside some of the team members as they empathized with what I portrayed as the terror inside this young man. "It is frightening to be so out of control," I told them. "It is frightening to know so much is at risk due to something inside that you don't want and can't identify or explain. It is awful to have such positive power and potential in so many aspects of your life, and to have within you the capacity to destroy it all without warning and without meaning to."

Feeling then that their empathy meant there was much room for growth for everyone, I had begun looking for a way to incorporate their emotional capacities into their role in Sam's life. Perhaps then, I had reasoned, they could trust and participate in a different, more successful approach than simply wanting Sam to comply. Even on that first day, I had begun the groundwork by explaining how Sam's rage-based behavior had formed, and then by expanding on the principles for reversing the rage.

"Because rage is the outcome of extreme unmet needs for love," I explained, "deep down in that condition is the extreme need for love. Therefore, its reversal is contingent on the person finally sensing that the need for love can be met.

"Anger is our emotional response when our needs are not met," is how I began describing the developmental process that leads to rage. "Love is our emotional response when our needs *are* met. The hidden message behind anger is, 'I need to feel more love.' And the rage is a cumulative condition resulting from the extreme experience of UnLove.

"A child can be in a loving environment, but that does not mean the child is *experiencing* the love," I said cautiously. "That is what the anger is trying to say. 'I need to feel more love, and I don't feel the *power* to attract the love I need. Instead, I'm using this extra-effort emotional energy inside me to try to get that message across, even though I don't necessarily *know* that's the message or the need inside me. If I knew that, I would say it directly. Instead, all I know is that I blow up and erupt without warning, without wanting to, despite trying to hold everything inside, and it's not working. In fact, it's getting worse. It's getting scarier and scarier inside me. I have these constant thoughts about what I might do. What I might say. What my life might end up like if I go on like this.'"

The Rage/Sadness Axis™

The rage, I explained, is a reservoir of accumulated anger, frozen in place by the fear that also has developed: the fear of not experiencing adequate love. The buildup of anger has continually driven love away, which is why the fear has developed. It is the fear of not having enough love, and the more anger accumulated, the greater the fear. At the same time, another consequence has developed. Sadness. Sadness is humanity's emotional response to the loss of love. Abusive, unpredictable anger results in the loss of love. Those outbursts drive the love away.

To explain how Sam's sadness was connected to the rage that these elders were trying to help with, I explained that the sadness had begun to accumulate long before they ever came into Sam's life. I knew these discussions about Sam would inevitably cause the team to think about their own childhoods—plus their own parenting experiences, their own children, and their own grandchildren. I assured them that in early life, the sadness that develops in children is not about what the children have done to create loss of love. It is about the *lack* of love, or the inadequacy of the love that is present.

The love may be there, but the love that is available is not touching or comforting or supporting them sufficiently. This is frightening for children in this type of environment. They know they need love. They know the love they *need* to feel is not available. Therefore, they create a strategy for surviving without adequate love. Sometimes children try to obtain love by pleasing others. Or they may create defense mechanisms to avoid the feelings resulting from needing and not experiencing adequate love. Whatever a child develops and locks into at this stage of emotional survival, the mechanisms are a testament to this scrappy little soul's power and creativity. At the same time, because these mechanisms are needed over and over again, they require instant reliability. As a result, they develop into automatic, instantly engagable patterns.

The patterns are dysfunctional because they are automatic. They also are dysfunctional because they are not emotionally integrated. Originally designed to shut off anger, fear, and sadness, the patterns activate and function in a manner that keeps all these emotions from surfacing. A tiny child's undeveloped emotional capacities are usually unable to accommodate the impact and implications of these developments. The prospects of living without adequate love are too painful and too frightening. Thus, the sadness that has developed has been suppressed since early life. It has been stored with a memory that says, "If I ever allow myself to feel this again, it will feel this unbearable, and I cannot survive it. Therefore, I must do whatever I can to avoid this feeling, and this vulnerability."

Rage is the condition that develops as a result. It has the power, and the function, to keep the child from re-experiencing the sadness that is stored below the surface. The problem is that rage is a cumulative *dys*functional condition in every manner. While it screams forth as an anguished, desperate cry for love, rage defies and protects fiercely from the source of ever experiencing love.

Until the sadness is released, the return to love cannot commence. And unless the rage relents, the loss of love persists. The resulting dysfunction is unavoidable and unstoppable because in the end, as an unintended consequence of avoiding sadness, rage ultimately destroys love.

Love, Rage and the Possibilities for Change

Sam was an intense example of the cumulative patterns and destruction of rage. His was also a situation that cried out for love on both sides. In agreeing to take on this enormous responsibility for this gifted/damaged young man, somehow this team of elders had derived their security and confidence almost entirely from a strategy based on dispassionate control.

It was ironic to be with them in meetings and hear their heart-felt commitment to Sam, but then experience such a departure, and disconnection, when I introduced the subject of increasing their own emotional adequacy. "Rage is a scream for love," I said to them a lot. "If we can create a different emotional response from *you*, the old patterns and grids within *him* will subside. Those patterns are based on his constant experience of his needs not being met. If that changes, so will his automatic responses."

It was difficult, however, to direct their attention to the underlying *emotional* patterns and needs that Sam's behavior reflected. The fact that none of them had experienced this behavior with any of their own children was undoubtedly one reason. But I kept sensing there was another, as well. I sensed that their confidence and adequacy lay in modeling good morals and values, setting boundaries, teaching consequences and discipline, and other traditional forms of successful upbringing.

From the beginning, this situation seemed to lack a capacity for these elders to truly *understand* that Sam was different, that his needs were different, and that the options he would respond to were different from what they knew to work in more traditional situations.

Lest a committed, practically exhausted parent, teacher, or elder read these portrayals of one complex situation and feel that I am implying fault or failure, I hasten to add that these individuals were truly heroic in many ways. Their unconditional commitment to Sam's situation was a blessing. It had perhaps saved his life. Although this situation had him locked up in one manner, it had undoubtedly saved him from lockup of a much more serious nature.

The problems in this situation were, in certain ways, more a mismatch. That is one of the reasons it reminded me of other families whose Indigo Children had said, "I don't feel like I belong here." Sam surely did not feel like he belonged in this situation. He frequently did not feel like he belonged anywhere, he told me once when we were alone. "Intellectually, I know these people love and care about me," he said. "I try to feel grateful. I try to act grateful. I try to be considerate, and act in other ways my parents taught me. But my guardians never give me anything I ask for. I only get what they think I need, or deserve. The only way they evaluate me is by my anger. They can't relate to any more of me than that."

"But do you show them that other side, Sam?" I asked. "Do you open up to them when you *are* feeling emotionally available and vulnerable? Do you offer them the experience of your other emotional options? Do you tell them what you need at a time and in a manner that enables them to *feel* your needs—and to have *feelings* about meeting your needs, or not meeting your needs? Or is it possible that you keep all those other feelings, except for the anger, inside?"

Thank goodness he spent some time thinking about that. And thank goodness Sam was emotionally honest. He acknowledged that he had stopped being open after a couple of months with his guardians. He had let them down, he said. They had gotten angry, and it felt like it used to feel when he was at home, so he had withdrawn. "I didn't know how to get back to where we used to be close. I didn't even know if that was possible. I just figured I had ruined everything, so I didn't try. My anger got worse, their response got worse, and that's the way it has continued. We are all doing the best we can, and that is pretty awful."

At that moment in this situation, I finally saw through the layers of patterns and grids. I saw how to work with the elders along the Love/Needs Axis™. Needs are the key to love, I reminded myself. The more love we have inside, the more love we have to share. I then began talking with the team about a collective exercise to open up some possibilities in their own relationship with love. That, I knew, would give them more creativity and flexibility in responding to Sam's needs. It would also increase their capacity to respond with more love.

It took some work, but it was the strategy that enabled them to yield and expand and establish a new track for interacting with Sam. The strategy was a bit too complex to describe in detail here, but the principles are important in helping other families in similar situations.

Principles for Increasing Emotional Potential

Principle 1: We, the elders, have untapped emotional potential. We are in these children's lives to help them develop emotional maturity and integration. But at the same time, the children are also an opportunity for us to expand. In even the most challenging situations, like the one with Sam, there is an opportunity on both sides to experience more love.

Principle 2: When our needs are met, our emotional capacities expand. There are many ways to feel love. The Love and Needs information in the *Transforming Anger Into Love*™ chapter is a reminder of the many ways to experience love by honoring our needs. One of the challenges for us, the elders, is to ensure that the choices and priorities in our own lives increasingly meet our own needs. In so doing, we continue to have sufficient love inside to be creative and adequate in meeting our children's needs.

Our children's anger is about needs that *we* have been unable to meet, based on our current capacities. However, with additional information and tools, we can often adequately *respond* to those needs, even though we may not be able to *meet* them on our own. Increasing our capacities often requires making changes within ourselves, and within our lives, that expand our capacities to meet and respond to our children's needs. Once we identify those changes and begin making those changes, we have a greater capacity to help our children attract whatever or whomever they additionally need.

Identifying and making the changes in our own lives is a major theme of this book. One of the reasons for that emphasis is that we are the ones closest to these children emotionally. We have the greatest responsibility, the greatest impact, and the greatest power to help them. The challenge is in increasing our capacities to do so.

Indigo Children's needs can be very intense, even demanding, and, at times, consuming. If from devotion or guilt or sheer non-consciousness we give and give and give and ignore our own needs and capacities, we can easily reach a point of gridlock. At that point, although we lack the power and creativity (*i.e.*, the capacity) to improve the situation, our needs lock us into the pattern of trying and usually exhausting ourselves, nevertheless.

Principle 3: If we lack the capacities to meet our own standards, or our commitments, we must renegotiate the situation and replenish ourselves based on our own needs. If we see that we are in such a pattern, trying and trying but not improving the situation, we must either renegotiate our commitment or increase our capacity.

This was a principle I finally realized the Sam situation urgently called for.

The Needs/Capacities Axis™

The minute Sam had described the pattern of his anger getting worse, the team's response getting worse, and the awful outcome, I realized that these elders had assumed this responsibility more from need than from capacity. And understandably. They wanted to help this young man and they wanted to help his family. They had competencies in many areas. In the beginning, there was no way to predict the changes Sam might undergo in a new environment. There was every reason to hope and expect that the changes everyone wanted would indeed come to pass. This team had been carefully assembled. It seemed to offer the spectrum of input Sam's situation would require. Its members were committed and confident.

But after a couple of months, when their emotional competency was not producing the changes they had envisioned, they did not know what else to do for this emotionally charged, emotionally challenging situation. In response to that, they focused on the power and control they *could* exert, both psychologically and physically.

Once I saw the patterns, the emotionally GridLocked developments made perfect sense to me. These elders did not have the emotional capacity or competency to address Sam's emotional condition and needs. This explained why they could not "give back," even though traditional behavior modification works both with consequences *and* rewards. These elders were not in touch with Sam's emotional needs. They were geared to address his emotional outbursts. Consequently, their collective emotional conscience did not say to them, "This is enough," or, "This hurts *me* too much. It can't be right. We've got to find another way. We've got to create some alternatives that feel good to us."

To increase their capacities in this situation required my helping them identify other areas of their lives where they felt limited, over-committed, or where their needs were not being met. For the patterns with Sam to have developed to this extent meant there were similar developments in the elders' own lives. Therefore, addressing only the patterns on Sam's side of the situation would have been futile. The patterns perpetuating the GridLock with Sam were fused to similar patterns functioning on the elders' side. They had to be. Otherwise, the discomfort from this situation as it developed would have been too great. The elders would not have allowed it.

They would have said, "This doesn't feel right," or "This does not meet my needs," or "I do not feel I am contributing. I must renegotiate and allow someone with different skills and expertise to come in." Instead, they dug in, just as they had done when challenged in certain ways in their own lives. Because this situation was familiar, they had not only allowed it to progress; they had even perpetuated it. As the manner in which this situation had developed began to match similar circumstances in their own lives, the elders had applied their past responses to this situation, as well. They had responded with, "Do more. Try harder. Don't give up. Don't give in."

To unlock this grid, I utilized an exercise much like the Needs Exercise in *Lifestyles of the Stressed and Strained*. I turned the focus completely away from Sam for a short time, and helped the elders focus on their own lives and their own needs. Some of them could not imagine how this would expand their capacities with Sam, but they followed the exercise anyway.

After completing the Needs Exercise, plus a few follow-up discussions, three members of the team renegotiated their agreement with the family. They identified the aspects of Sam they enjoyed, and volunteered to be with him under those conditions. But they asked not to be responsible for solving the anger problems any more. They had reached their limit, they realized. What they needed was to be available in the ways that felt good to them, and to be relieved of the responsibilities that did not.

For Sam, the guardians, and the remainder of the team, this was great news. The elders whom Sam especially liked were free to be with him in ways that they, too, could enjoy. Their contribution to the situation was no longer limited to being part of the team. They could be mentors. They could have personal, one-on-one time with this delightful young man. The limitations of the former arrangement no longer constricted anyone. There was finally new potential and new hope.

The Anger/Love Axis™

Duplicating exactly what worked with Sam's team is certainly not the only solution to such seemingly intractable situations. For parents and teachers, it's certainly not about resigning from the team. It's about resigning from these kinds of patterns. The ones where we trudge ahead, committed and exhausted, improving very little, and despairing quite a lot.

Resigning from the patterns requires first that we identify them, then admit to them, and finally, honor the responsibility to replenish ourselves in the wake of them. Replenishing ourselves is especially important in a situation where we feel we are not being competent and effective. An unproductive pattern is at work when we are not experiencing an internal reward for our efforts—a reward that registers somehow in the form of love.

As parents and teachers, feeling that we are not being competent and effective can be our experience almost every day. Our tendency often is to resign ourselves to the idea that there is nothing more we can do and nothing more we can change, possibly because we feel we have already tried everything and nothing in the situation has budged. So we get up the next day and face the same circumstances and try to make the best of it again. In the process, we further descend into the pattern of giving without replenishing.

This pattern does not meet our needs for balance and self-nurturing. It does not meet our need to experience meaningful results from our efforts. On some level, the same pattern that is increasing our frustration and depletion is also activating our anger. If we honored the anger and the unmet needs it represents, we would not perpetuate the patterns. The problem is that many of us do not honor our anger, which in turn means that our needs do not get met. So, we lock into automatic patterns, which are a hapless effort to try and get our needs met. Unfortunately, by then—by the time the patterns have formed—we are so far removed from our own needs that the best we can do is try to feel reward from meeting others' needs.

With children, that's easy to do. We haven't replenished ourselves in so long, however, we don't have the extra capacity to do for others. We have the *need* to do for them, so we try, but our efforts are inadequate, and we can't sustain them. Then our inadequacy makes the others feel abandoned and angry. So we try harder to meet their needs without meeting ours. And so it goes.

Anger: Its Purpose and Function

Although the purpose of anger is to produce change, we often neglect tapping the capacities within ourselves as the most direct, powerful force for change. As an example not related to Sam, let's look at a common stressor for children and families. Homework. Some schools require huge amounts of homework in subjects that our gifted children find boring and useless. It can be heartbreaking to insist that they sit in their rooms studying four or five nights a week. Because the school they want to go to requires a certain grade point average, however, we tend to push and coax and assure them that the hours and the grades will be worth it.

With several more weeks of this stressful routine looming ahead, it would almost never occur to a parent to say, "All right. I can't do anything about the school lesson plans, but what I *can* do is arrange for childcare one Saturday night a month and go to the theater. That will feed my soul. It will give me a break. It will inspire me, and it will add to my capacities for being supportive and available to my children."

The Anger/Love Axis™ is our principal indicator when we either have the capacity or we have lost the capacity to be effective in behalf of someone we love. The indicators on each end of this axis will activate accordingly. We will either love and feel reward for how we are being, or we will resent and feel discouraged and depleted.

In the situation with Sam, the guardians and the team assembled to help them were in his life as a result of love. Their anger and frustrations indicated that the situation was not meeting their needs. Their anger was an indication that something had to change. Their options were to (1) make changes in the situation, or (2) make some types of changes within themselves. Their anger was not creating desired positive changes in the situation because it was not expressed. It was, in an indirect way, causing change in the situation, however, as the number of amenities in Sam's life changed (*e.g.*, diminished). The other dynamic along the Anger/Love Axis™ is based not only on the purpose of anger (to create change), but also on the function of anger: to challenge love to expand.

The changes this situation was undergoing were not increasing the experience or supply of love for either side. That meant there was an automatic unproductive pattern reproducing the same, ineffective, limiting results. If we recognize this development in our own lives, it is an indicator that the change we need is to add to our own capacities. Then we will have more to offer the situation. If we cannot add to our capacities, we must renegotiate based on what we know to be our (perhaps dwindling) capacities and our (likely increasing) needs for change.

Trusting this axis means trusting our anger. In the Sam situation, this first meant unearthing the anger. As the Needs Exercise with Sam's team got underway, it revealed a considerable amount of anger that none of the team members had ever expressed, either to the guardians or to the other members. Unaware of how their suppressed anger held certain unproductive, limiting patterns in place, they had been both unwilling and unable to express their anger.

"I didn't know it mattered," one member finally admitted.

"I didn't even know I was angry," another realized.

The insight that may be most helpful to parents, teachers, and those who are closest to the Indigo Children's needs and situations came, thankfully, from one of the guardians.

"I knew I was frustrated. I knew I had to keep a grip on the situation. I knew the more Sam rebelled, the more resolved I was to showing him that he had to be better behaved in order to be successful in the world. But I never realized I was only using my anger. I thought his behavior triggered my commitment. I never realized my anger triggered his anger, and that his anger triggered mine. I thought I was showing love by setting boundaries and teaching him to be responsible. I was enforcing rules so he could stay out of jail.

"Although what we were doing wasn't working, I didn't ever think it was our anger. I only thought it was his."

Self-Health and Anger

So many of us who are elders grew up being told it wasn't nice to be angry. We soon figured out that being nice meant experiencing approval and love. Stuffing anger, therefore, meant experience approval and love. So we stuffed our anger. Along that same developmental path, some of us experienced others' abuse and rage, and we fervently promised ourselves we would never be like that. In those types of environments, we did not learn how to use anger in an effective way. We did not even learn how to recognize some of its passive, subtle formats. Instead, we learned to deny or suppress anger—or to fear it. In some ways, as a result, we became just like the people we promised ourselves we would never be like.

Although we may not have become overtly abusive, if our anger is in any way troubling to us as elders, we most likely still carry the residue of early-life conditioning.

Anger forms pernicious patterns. It sabotages even the best of intentions and plans. We can know our children are losing trust as we vacillate between being understanding and supportive one day, short-tempered and unavailable the next. We can sense them creating distance, and we can cry and feel guilty and redouble our efforts to ask more questions, and to be better at keeping our word. But all that planning and commitment can be eclipsed in a flash. One harsh remark can pierce a known sensitive place or an inner sanctuary recently shared and instantly: "It's over!"

Not everything, and not forever, thank heavens. But those are the unavoidable, uncontrollable, uncalculated consequences of anger when it's been suppressed and denied.

In Sam's situation, it was not what they said that was so counterproductive. In this situation, the people gathered in his behalf did *not* say they were getting frustrated or that they needed a change. They also had no idea their unexpressed anger was contributing to the patterns and grids they kept encountering. This is true in many circumstances with children who have powerful emotions and needs. Elders do everything they can to help with their children's anger, often unaware of how their own anger, whether *ex*pressed or *sup*pressed, is holding the children's patterns in place.

The following are guidelines I shared with Sam's team. They are likely to be helpful in any situation that is not improving, or is getting worse despite considerable efforts by committed, loving individuals.

Understanding Anger: Avoiding Rage

Anger

Anger is a God-given emotion. It is a proportional, loving emotion. Anger is more intense than love is. Therefore, during an angry exchange, the anger may be dominant, but underneath that anger is love. The presence of love is, in fact, the principal distinction between anger and rage. When we love our self as we express anger, and love what we say and do as we express anger, our anger will return us to love.

If we lose touch with love while we are expressing anger, that is a signal to immediately stop what we are saying and doing and return to the self and the behavior that we can love. Too many episodes of not doing so put our emotional health and integrity at risk. Too much unloving anger is a developmental indicator of anger progressing into rage.

Rage

Rage is a dysfunctional, destructive emotional condition that has the capacity to destroy love, both within our self and in all aspects of our life. Rage lacks emotional conscience. At the time it is engaged, it is completely out of touch with love. It so severely ravages a person of the experience of love that the person's intense *need* for love can sometimes be confused as the capacity to feel and offer love. The person can disguise this need as capacity, and another emotionally needy person can mistake this need for capacity. However, the desperation of each person's needs, combined with the truth of each person's emotional inadequacies, soon become evident. And potentially destructive.

Sometimes, following the rage, a person can feel a sense of guilt or regret. But until the rage is successfully reversed, those feelings are unsustainable. They follow the most recent incident of lost love, but they do not flow from the presence of love within. Therefore, those responses of guilt and regret are inadequate to penetrate the patterns and grids of the rage. In a matter of time, therefore, this condition of emotional dysfunction will resume, and the extreme, uncontrollable outcome will repeat.

Love

Love is the enduring emotion. Love and anger co-exist. When anger is allowed to build up inside to the degree it loses its proportionality, anger is not safe. It puts our relationship with love at risk. Anger is a message about needs. If our needs are not met, our love does not expand. Losing proportionality is a warning sign that our suppressed anger is also losing its integrity. In some aspects of our life, we are not being honest about what we feel and what we need. We are manipulating our anger by suppressing it and allowing it to build. At the point of recognizing that, we must assess our needs and the choices we are making in our life and increase our experience and supply of love.

If anger is expressed at the time and to the degree it is felt, it is discharged into a situation to disrupt whatever isn't meeting our needs. Ideally, the anger then rearranges the situation so it does meet our needs. Depending on the quality and quantity of love within us, we can often absorb anger. Then we do not have to express it. We may feel the anger rise; but if the love within us responds sufficiently, we can allow the person or situation to "be." Then our capacity to be patient, understanding, and compassionate can override the anger. That is the purpose of learning about anger. In so doing, we can expand our experience of love.

Self-Love

Anger expands our experience of love. If we discharge it into a situation and the change that results meets our needs, we feel more love. If we respond with love from within and transform the anger, that too increases our experience of love: self-love. Even more astounding is the experience of self-love that comes from being honest about what we feel and what we need. Although we may not obtain the change we need in the outer circumstances, we have added to the love inside by having the courage and integrity to express the truth. "I am angry. This is what I am angry about. This is the change I need."

Then anger maintains its integrity and fulfills its purpose: to create change. It has been utilized, it has been released, and it can then be replaced by love. This is not only a healthy way to express our own anger. It is also the model for helping us understand and manage our children's anger.

Take Away's: What Works, What Doesn't, and Why

Expressing our anger does not ensure our needs will be met. It does not guarantee that anything in the outer environment will change. It does increase our self-love, however, and it does prevent us from building up a reservoir of unexpressed anger that can turn into rage. For our children's sake, it is important for them to learn, from experiencing our own emotional integrity, that anger is not an unloving emotion; that anger and love co-exist.

The presence of love enables children to trust anger. The presence of love is also the measure of when our anger is safe and productive. In the situation with Sam, if the take away's had been accomplished with love, he would not have felt so stripped. The privileges may have been gone, but the love would have remained with him. As it was, his guardians admitted that they were usually angry when they took away his phone, his boom box, his television, or his VCR—and that their anger was not expressed with love.

Since take away's are often a part of discipline, it is the accompaniment of love that makes them effective. A classic example is that developmental moment when a young one discovers how to open the kitchen cabinet and sees all those pots and pans. Perhaps this first happens on a day when the parent is able to accommodate the clanging and disarray, and even delight in witnessing it. The next day, that little one is likely to head back to that same cabinet and do that same thing; and do it a few more times. Then the time comes when the clanging and putting up pots and pans is no longer a parent's delight.

It does *not* meet the parent's need at this stage, so the parent attempts to redirect the child's attention. But that doesn't work. In fact, several times it may not work. By now, the parent urgently needs a boundary. The child, however, has settled in to a routine.

With thousands of these types of transactions throughout the course of parenting, we undoubtedly respond many, many times with patience and love. But at other times, we may not have that patience, and unconditional love may not be our first response. We may be inclined to simply take something away instead of seeing this as a negotiating, or teaching opportunity. If we take away as a last resort, or from emotional powerlessness, or an out-of-control state, the take-away action makes matters worse.

When we take away with our self-love engaged, we love how we behave as we negotiate, or prevail. With young Indigo Children, this is especially important. In the beginning of this chapter, the grandmother named Kitty said it well. "They will learn, but only with love." Indigo Children have superior emotional intelligence. They sense the instant our emotions change, especially to something other than love. Unwittingly some times, very purposefully at others, their inclination is to do something to disrupt whatever unproductive emotional state we are in, and prompt us to focus back to the love. When their anger engages in this manner, the following guidelines can help.

- **"I can see that you are angry."**
- **"I hear your anger."**
- **"I realize you are angry."** These responses acknowledge the child's anger. They signal to the child that the anger has gotten your attention. That is the first step toward the anger producing more love.

- **"Are you feeling angry right now?"** helps the child learn to recognize anger, and to discover that it is an acceptable emotion when expressed at the time and in the manner it can be productive.

- **"What do you need?"** honors the purpose of the anger: to produce change.
- **"What can I do to help?"** is the option that extends love.

The latter two, "What do you need?" and "What can I do to help?" are especially powerful acknowledgments of the child's anger and needs. But equally powerful is that we be emotionally available for the answer. It is important to wait, in silence, until the child responds. Pelting the child with more questions is usually counterproductive at this time. It signifies our need (and impatience, perhaps). It is not creating the opportunity for us to hear and adequately respond to the child's need. In such an exchange, the child's anger may finally be coming to the surface because we asked the critical question: "What do you need?"

Generally, anger has been suppressed because of the child's experience and/or conditioning. The child concludes, "You aren't available, or adequate to meet my needs. Therefore, I won't continue trying to express my needs (with my anger). I'm getting the opposite of what I need when I try to let you know what I need, so I'll stop expressing my needs (with the emotional response designed to signify my needs: my anger). I can stop expressing my anger. The problem is, I can't stop needing what I need."

By finally asking, "What do you need?" you have created an opening that is of huge significance. It may take a few moments for the child to respond. The child may need time to emotionally *process* this important moment, in addition to needing time to get in touch with the need you are finally asking about. If we listen, and the child expresses the need but we cannot meet the child's need at the moment, or even ever, it is important to say that, with love. "I'm truly sorry I can't do that right now." Or, "I'm sorry that I can't be that for you." Or, "I don't know what to do to help right now."

With Indigo Children especially, it always helps them to understand why. Then, if we also ask them to help us come up with something that *will* meet their needs, we will be both grateful for and impressed with their own creative solutions.

Thank You, Sam

I often think of that first meeting with Sam's team. I remember feeling, how wonderful that they, too, will be able to release some of the controlled and controlling aspects within themselves. How wonderful that they, too, will be able to replace some of their conditioned responses with a greater emotional security and power within. How wonderful that there are principles for Transforming Anger Into Love.™ I am profoundly grateful to know these principles. I have seen them work hundreds and hundreds of times. I therefore spoke confidently and knowingly at that first meeting with the guardians and team, although I left out one large piece of the whole of what I knew Sam was going through.

I am including it here because this not only gives a fuller picture of this particular young man's untapped emotional intelligence and potential. It also is an example of the enormous human capacities that are often trapped beneath protective patterns and grids.

"When I *am* calm enough to think about all this," Sam said, "I think, why don't they see how desperate I am? Why can't they figure out what I'm only occasionally able to see for myself—but which they ought to be able to see! Don't they see that this behavior isn't part of some grand plan I have for making myself miserable and taking everyone else down with me? Don't they see that I just become more of a zombie the more they try to control me? The more they take things away from me? Don't they see that I just dig down inside myself and somehow come up with whatever it takes to pretend I don't care; that I can live without *any*thing?"

Then, toward the end of this lengthy description of his circumstances, Sam asked with an expression I will never forget, "Don't they see it's a power play that we're both losing?"

These elders had given, and been through, so much. Often besieged by worry and fear, they had paced the floors many sleepless nights, and had driven around looking for Sam countless times when he didn't come home. They had also developed health problems so serious that two of them had to begin taking medication. I wanted to share with you these few select observations and examples from this most complex and rewarding situation because it so inspiringly depicted the ultimate possibilities. In the beginning it was about restriction, power, and control. But in the end, it was about options, needs, and growth.

As all of us continue to find our way through the challenges of similar situations, it is important to remember that, just as Doreen Virtue's powerful book of information and insights is titled, the "care and feeding of Indigo Children" is a work in progress. The information, delineations, and how-to's are just now gathering. Whether we are parents, siblings, family, friends, teachers, professionals, adult Indigos, or the Children themselves, this is a body of work that will take time and patience, grace and commitment, to assemble and to master.

In addition, as other professionals suggest, and I certainly agree, these children are in our lives to teach us and to cause us learn new emotional options and potential. As we seek guidance in helping them, we inevitably discover insights that will add to our own capacities. This is undoubtedly part of the Indigo Children's purpose. This book is, therefore, devoted not only to more effectively managing these children's emotional patterns. It is designed to contribute to our own emotional competency and adequacy, as well.

Indigo Children are, after all, very dynamic, challenging, powerful, and knowing young Beings. They require us to use our love and creativity to identify additional outlets for their exceptional intellect and creativity. It follows that they will offer similar challenges and need additional resources at the emotional level, as well.

In the chapter that includes an interview with Melanie Melvin, Ph.D., her extensive and successful use of homeopathy confirms that homeopathic remedies can be an extremely effective resource to complement the emotional needs and conditions in Indigo Children. In the three books mentioned previously in this text, many, many valuable resources are discussed. These books are essential reading for anyone who wants to know more about the presence of these children's gifts, and the gift of these children's presence.

In the meantime, I am certain we are all doing the best we can. I do not know one parent or guardian, family member or friend, teacher, counselor, practitioner, or Indigo Child, who does not do everything possible to achieve all the love and support and positive change within each one's capacity. This challenge is immeasurable for all of us who know these children and feel some calling or capacity to add to the literature, to the conversation, and to the exchange of what works, what doesn't, who has expertise and suggestions, remedies and research, methodologies and models.

My contribution happens to be about the anger. It is one I offer with immense gratitude, and love.

Notes

Chapter Three

44 Ways To Show Kids You Care

While these guidelines are for all children and all families, some are especially important for Indigo Children. As parents, teachers, professionals, and anyone who knows or works with Indigo Children knows, these children have questions and make observations we ordinarily associate with adult maturity and competency. Therefore, it is important to give Indigos the developmental support and cues their ages and vulnerabilities require, yet do so in a manner that honors their wisdom, sensitivity, and intellect. What a wonderful opportunity and challenge!

Other teachers and professionals have offered numerous helpful and profound insights throughout the Indigo Books. A few of those are included at the end of this chapter.

44 Ways To Show Kids You Care

1. Say the word "love" a lot.
2. Be careful not to criticize; simply tell them a better way.
3. If you withdraw your attention, avoid withdrawing your love.
4. Teach the principles of "why," not just "what" to do or not do.
5. Discipline with love, especially if you are angry. If you "punish" or "take away," do so with love and follow up with love.

6. Remember that children often reflect what they have or have not been taught. They often need to be taught, not punished.

7. Teach children to trust the truth by experiencing you as a model of the truth, and a model of loving them for telling the truth.

8. Be patient, not just tolerant.

9. Ask them what they need from you and do whatever you can to meet those needs.

10. When you are stressed and unavailable, help them know that your condition is about *your* life, not them, and reaffirm your love.

11. Remember that children often need love the most when they "deserve" it the least.

12. Listen to them, a lot. Avoid interrupting.

13. Help them learn the feeling of regret, not just to say they are sorry.

14. Apologize when you make a mistake or do something you regret.

15. Teach them about ethics and values and principles they can apply in choices and decision-making.

16. Never make fun of them, shame them, or blame them. It's not their "fault." It's an indication of what they need, or what they need to learn, or what they need to unlearn.

17. Tell them how much you like being with them, if you mean it. If you don't, examine what about the relationship dynamics at that moment or in general affects your *not* feeling that way. Then find a way to change that from within yourself.

18. Expect and support their best; don't expect or require perfection. Set standards based on their capacities, not your (often unrealistic) needs.

19. Avoid comparing them to anyone else; instead, help them develop their unique self and way of being.

20. Know that they will respect what you say if they respect who you are.

21. Encourage them to share and teach them to share but don't make them share. If they feel enough love in their life they will be able to share; if they cannot share, it means they need to feel more love.

22. Hug and touch them often when they are young. Hug and touch

them as often as possible as they mature. Avoid commands like, "Come, give me a hug." Instead, say, "I would like to hug. Would *you* like to hug?" The command is based on the adult's need. The option is contingent on the child's need.

23. Help them learn the feeling of gratitude, not just to say thank you. Love is the emotion that sustains positive change. Anger is the emotion that sabotages positive change.

24. Give them space when they need it.

25. Praise more and criticize less.

26. Know that a child experiencing love will express love. A child who does not act loving needs to experience more love and feel more loved. Until then, behavior changes you attempt may not be sustainable.

27. Help them learn how and why to save money.

28. Avoid emphasizing how much something costs.

29. Help them discover what has meaning and purpose and feels good to them.

30. Keep the promises you make. If you do not keep your word, acknowledge that. Help them understand the circumstances or choices that precipitated the change. They will notice if this becomes a pattern.

31. Answer their questions.

32. If you do not like their friends, teach them the qualities to look for in friends.

33. Go to their games and events; get to know their teachers and coaches.

34. Be consistent.

35. Let them tell you how they feel. Help them learn what their feelings are and how to express them.

36. Give them lots of compliments, and mean it. If you do not / cannot compliment them, examine why.

37. Suggest better behaviors when they act out. Teach first. Reward often. Be understanding. Punish last.

38. When they withdraw, offer love instead of demands or threats.

39. Nurture them with good food, prepare their favorite foods, and help them make good nutritional choices.

40. Teach them to be responsible according to their own developmental age; avoid using them to do tasks that are *your* responsibility.

41. When you notice behavioral changes, be especially available so they can talk about what is going on.

42. Be understanding when they have a difficult day.

43. Teach them to be on time and to keep their word and their commitments—and model that for them.

44. Love them no matter what. If you are feeling love for them at the time you express anger, your anger is safe. Otherwise, they experience anger as having the power to displace love. Then they will learn to fear anger—yours *and* their own—and potentially develop the pattern of suppressing anger, which in sufficient accumulation, can turn into rage.

Also Keep In Mind...

From Melanie Melvin, Ph.D.:[1]

- "It's better to hear out their reasons and then consider carefully before answering. If you say no and then relent, they will quickly learn to keep pestering until they get their way. This does not mean you should give them everything they want; just mean what you say when you answer yes or no to their request.

- "If you are concerned or have some nutritional information to offer, share it with them. Then back off and let them make their own choices. Their body's wisdom will tell them what they need much more clearly if they are not contaminated with fads and fears, shoulds and shouldn'ts."

From Judith Spitler McKee, Ed.D.:[1]

- "Children develop trust as they learn in their bodies and spirits that their basic physical, emotional, intellectual, and creative needs will be met by the caregivers and special adults in their lives. The messages sent and care given by adults must be more pleasant than painful, and more love-based than fear-based. From trust, a tapestry is woven of mutuality, connectedness, and respect between adults and children.

- "Adults sometimes use techniques of shaming and inducing guilt because that is what they remember from their own childhoods. These highly injurious techniques *seem* to work because children do act differently when shamed, especially if it is done in public. Actually these techniques do *work*, but at a major cost to the child's developing personality! Shame and unnecessary guilt negatively affect the child's quest for individual expression. Shame and guilt are such powerful and painful emotions that they often block curiosity, play, and creativity. Children quickly learn to not be open or honest with others."

From Kathy McCloskey, Ph.D.:[1]

- "Give these children adult explanations.
- They will catch you in all deceptions.
- They not only know who *they* are, they also know who *you* are. When you love them and recognize who they are, they will open to you like no other.
- If you say you love them, but treat them in a disrespectful way, they will not trust you.
- They will not believe you love them if you do not treat them in a loving way. All the words in the world will fall on deaf ears.
- The way you conduct your own life and 'run' your own family is direct evidence to the Indigo Child about whether you are loving or not!"

From Cathy Patterson, special education teacher:[1]

- "Parents do not help their children by explaining that they are 'Indigo Children' and then allowing them to misbehave without boundaries and guidelines. Even children who could eventually raise the consciousness of the planet need boundaries. With boundaries, self-control is learned, which is integral for a peaceful community.
- "Remember to always be consistent even if you feel that you don't have the energy to follow your discipline plan. Otherwise, children learn that they don't need to follow rules, because those rules are always changing."

From Debra Hegerle, Indigo mother and teacher's aide:[1]

- "Indigos are open and honest—this is not a vulnerability, but their greatest strength. If you are not open and honest with them, they will still be so with you; however, they will not respect you. That's a serious issue with Indigos… If they notice that there is a hidden motive behind your attempt to get them to do something, they will resist strongly and feel perfectly justified in doing so. From their point of view, if you're not doing your work in the relationship, they can challenge you on it.

- "They're working to help us adults to help us recognize where we are holding and using old, subtle patterns to manipulate them, which used to work but will no longer. So if you are constantly getting resistance from an Indigo, check yourself first. They may be holding up a mirror for you.

- "Boredom can bring out arrogance in Indigos so don't let them get bored."

From Barbra Gilman, parent and therapist:[2]

- "… allow them to experience natural consequences rather than punishment or rewards.

- "They do not under any circumstances respond well to lies, manipulation, or violence. …they instinctively know the greatest secret: Peace begins at home."

From Robert C. Ocker, teacher:[1]

- "Punishment will not work with these kids. It establishes fear, requires judgment, creates intentions of anger, and invites more conflict. These children will withdraw, rebel, and sink inward with hate. This is dangerous for their souls and for the lives of others. Avoid punishment!

   Discipline guides children by providing logical and realistic consequences. It shows what they have done wrong, gives them ownership of the problem, offers them ways to solve the problem they created, and leaves their dignity intact.

   Experiencing logical and realistic consequences teaches the

Indigo Child that they have positive control over their lives and that they can make decisions and solve their own problems. The children want this guidance. It empowers their royal and wise nature and gives them the power to be responsible, resourceful, and caring individuals. It allows them to be Who They Are!

These children demand dignity and worth. They read your intent more than your words. They are wise in their souls, young in their hearts."

Notes

Chapter Four

Transforming Anger Into Love™

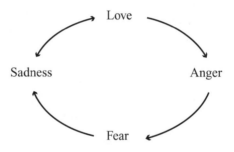

An Overview of the Four Basic Emotions

Because anger is the focus of the principles for Transforming Anger Into Love™, it is helpful to know the unique purpose and function of each of the four basic human emotions. That will assist you in understanding the complex properties and interactions of anger as it impacts fear, sadness, and love. In this overview of the four emotions you will learn how they interact, how they complement one another, the individual purpose and function of each, and how each emotion is designed to enrich our experience of life.

When we *suppress* our emotions, they do not enrich our life. Denying or "stuffing" emotions creates consequences. It allows that suppressed emotional energy to build up and be released in excess, usually taking a cumulative toll inside us (as stress and dis-ease) as well. Almost every page of this book, therefore, has something to say about expressing rather than suppressing emotions. The reason is that suppression is the first step toward extreme emotional dysfunction… the kind that turns inwardly into depression, and outwardly into rage.

There are ways to prevent rage from accumulating. There even are ways to reverse it. That is the most hopeful message about Transforming Anger Into Love™. It offers a joyful, inspiring journey to emotional well-being. It is an experience that begins and ends with love.

I. Love: The Enduring Emotion

Love is the creative emotion. It creates life itself. In an ideal world we would all experience sufficient love to create a meaningful, fulfilling, prosperous life. Then anger would not be necessary. In many ways, that is the purpose of all the principles and information in this book. If we can eliminate the patterns of suppressing anger, we can eliminate the principal obstacle to experiencing love.

Because love is our emotional response when our needs are met, the more capably we navigate our life in relation to our needs, the more love we feel inside. "But what if I don't know what my needs are?" people often ask. Or they say, "I know many of my needs that don't get met. But with a family, two kids, and a job, I've given up. It just isn't going to happen."

That may be true for many people reading this book. In the *Lifestyles of the Stressed and Strained* chapter, I discuss why our own needs are so important. They are, after all, critically linked to our experience and supply of love. So when we give and give to the others in our life, but find reasons for not resupplying love to ourselves, the result is exhaustion—emotional and physical. Then we are unable to meet our children's needs. And that is a likely setup for The Anger Grid™.

The more love we feel, the more love we have to give, and the more love we attract. That's even true in our role as parents and teachers. If the children are cranky and close to "pushing our buttons," we know the difference when we respond from love rather than anger. The love we offer helps calm them and redirect or reduce their frustrations and demands. We can't offer that option, however, if our own needs have not resupplied the love within us. The more love we feel inside, the greater our capacity to engage patience, understanding, forgiveness, humor, creativity, renegotiation, and other healthy alternatives to anger.

Self-Love: Where It All Begins

These days, many of us plead for healthy alternatives to our anger when it comes to kids and their music. I do not have a universal solution, but I can offer some important principles to keep in mind. For example, let's say you've asked your teenager repeatedly to keep the volume down and she doesn't. You have warned and threatened and are planning to take drastic action when one day she comes home from school and you can tell something is really bothering her. She rushes to her room and starts up the music, and you just know it's an effort to drown out the pain.

You also know you are about to drown in the aggravation. But then you stop. You think about her feelings, her day, and her need for this music right now. Instead of getting angry again, you take time to focus on your love for her. You recall precious moments: her first words, her birthdays, her excitement with school projects, and the immeasurable joy she has brought to your life. After a few minutes reminiscing, do you yell at her to turn down the music? No. You create patience and understanding from that supply of love inside you, and ask her if there is anything you can do to help.

Another day all you may be able to do is turn on your own music or TV or straighten up the garage, again. In a different frame of mind, you might listen to the words she's turning to. Yes, it's a grating, jarring offense to your ears. But there's a need there. There's a message, too. Love is the creative emotion. It creates alternatives and options within us.

If a pattern is developing between us and our child—a recurring anger that creates emotional distance—our staying angry, or becoming more angry, or retreating with the insulation of our own anger in place is not taking us in the direction our child needs. We know this, deep down inside. It never feels good to withdraw in anger, or to hold onto anger. We don't feel good when we know our child is in distress, but we have our own stress to deal with, so we think, "I have to take care of myself right now. I simply cannot risk knocking on her door and saying, 'Let's talk.'"

Love Heals

We can, however, break this kind of pattern. We can hold in our awareness this moment of her need that we can't fulfill and our anger that we can't shake. We can also value reclaiming our emotional connection with her as soon as possible, because the anger-based patterns that breach our children's emotional security develop one transaction at a time... on both sides.

Anger is always a message about love. The degree of the anger matches the need to feel love. The hidden message behind anger is, "I need to feel more love." Sometimes our own frustration takes over and we forget that we are neglecting the love needs that only we can meet. For those and many more reasons, it is important to monitor how long we stay angry, how often we are angry, how often the anger is recurring with us and our child... and to make certain we always return to the love as soon as we possibly can. Doing so is important to our emotional well-being, and it is essential to theirs.

The guideline to follow is "return to the love as soon as possible." Sometimes we really have to struggle to do so. But if we don't even hold this in our minds, and value it more than anything else in our hearts, then the anger can build and take over before we realize it has done so. The more love we have inside us to draw from, the greater our options for responding from love instead of anger when these episodes occur. The more love we have inside, the sooner we can return to the love when they do occur. And the more our life is meeting our own needs, the more available and capable we are to meet our children's needs... for love.

As one last guideline for these moments, think of the scenario when you've "had it" with your little one and you utter emphatically, "Go to your room and stay there until dinner." It's five o'clock and your regular dinner hour is six. He does go to his room. You do hear his sobs, and after 20 minutes the pain inside you is awful. "It's important to keep my word," you say over and over to yourself. And that is true. However, anger is a complex emotion, and following its cues is a complex task.

One reliable set of principles is that anger is a God-given emotion. It is proportional. It is meted out in the quality and quantity of energy that is perfect to serve its purpose: to make the change in the supply of love. In addition, the function of anger is to expand our connection with love—

and love is the enduring emotion. Love is also the emotion that heals. Therefore, when the anger has done its work and the love returns, there is nothing more the anger can do. At that moment, it's time for the love to do *its* work.

At that time, I suggest, it is more important to act on the love that has gathered inside you than to act on the anger that has long since passed. The exchange from anger to love lets you know you and your child now need to experience love. It has taken 20 minutes for the anger to do all it can do. An additional 40 minutes of feeling punished and alienated and unloved can be counterproductive for your child. That is what your love is telling you. Trust it. Go up to his room and use your love to discuss the incident with him. Let him know you feel awful. Let him know there are consequences to what he did that merited being sent to his room. Let him know you are fully prepared for him to spend another 40 minutes in his room in order to learn the lesson. But help him learn also how love works in connection with anger. Love is, after all, the greatest teacher.

We create self-love by doing what is good for us.

Because anger patterns like the ones discussed previously are so familiar, we may often ask ourselves:

- What enables me to be patient and understanding sometimes, but yelling and out of control at other times?
- What is the difference between *wanting* to honor my child's needs, but not having that capacity and flexibility inside myself?
- What are some ways to reduce the anger and tension that inevitably erupt between my child and me?

These types of questions are answered in several ways throughout this book. The words to look for are "self-love." It determines our capacity to express love for others.

In our culture we learn to say, "I love you." What is more accurate is to say, "I love the feeling inside me that is activated by your presence." The only love we can feel is within.

Even though we may know that, and may know that self-love is the answer to having a better relationship with our children (and also with others), we may not know how to create more self-love. Here, then, are a few simple principles and suggestions.

Each of us has our own standards and values. They contribute to our uniqueness and growth. For example, some of us are to eat health foods. Others are to shop for the best food bargains. Some of us are to maintain rigorous exercise. Others go walking or practice yoga. Some families choose a job requiring travel because the salary is necessary for the kids' educational needs. For other families, that would be unthinkable. Time together in the formative years is a priority, no matter what.

Although the self-love how-to's may seem to vary considerably, the consistent measure is the answer to, "What do I know to be good for *me*?" One day it may be good for us to skip our walk to have quality time with our children by driving them to school. Another day that same choice could be co-dependent. It could play into a needy pattern a child is on the verge of developing. It could also lead to an unproductive pattern on our part—always putting the kids' needs first.

As we learn about self-love, it is important to recognize that self-love is not self-ish. Self-love is the presence of love. Self-ish is based on the need for love. When we have self-love within, we have love to offer. When we need love, we can be self-ish.

It is unlikely any of us can make self-loving choices every time. Life is just too complex. We can, however, look for patterns that build up and take us away from too many of the choices we know to be good for us. Our anger is one way to tell if such patterns are underway. Anger tells us when our lives are not meeting our needs. Since the purpose of anger is to create change, it nudges us to make some changes in our choices and priorities. If we do that early enough, the self-love we experience as a result of making good choices will avoid the buildup of patterns so powerful we have to use anger to break free of them.

We compromise self-love when we do what is not good for us.

- We love the self that is honest and accountable. We erode self-love when we lie, avoid and deceive.
- We love having the courage to be honest about what we feel and what we need. We do not like the aspect of our self that is afraid to say what we feel. We do not like the aspect that forfeits its own needs in order to please someone else.
- We love the self that can manage money, manage time, keep its

word, and honor its commitments. We compromise self-love when we are excessive and undisciplined, when we promise more than we can deliver, and when we manipulate others into meeting our needs.

- We love the maturity within the self that says no to a situation that is tempting, but not the best choice. We lose self-respect when we yield to people or situations because we want to be liked, or when we say yes because we are afraid to say no.

- We love the self that maintains balance and order. When we let things pile up, our self-worth goes down.

- We love the self that sets realistic goals. We lose trust in the self who commits based on needs rather than capacities.

- We love the self that is focused and accomplishes what it sets out to do. When distractions and interruptions constantly sabotage our plans, we feel powerless and out of control. Those feelings diminish self-love.

- We love the self that expresses its potential. We resent the habits and patterns we develop that restrict that full, joyful expression.

Love and Needs

Love is our emotional response when our needs are met. It is the foundation and security for expressing our potential. Since the presence of love is connected with needs, increasing our experience of love requires knowing and meeting our needs. Needs not only tell us what is good for us, they tell us what is us, and they distinguish us from everyone else.

Knowing our needs is essential. Loving and valuing them, however, can be difficult. Because needs are so complex, efforts to change them or disregard them can sometimes make matters worse. What does help is to understand the purpose and message of needs. Aside from the primary needs for food, clothing, shelter, and safety, all the other needs are in some way connected to love. But that, too, is a complex subject. There is more than one type of love, and more than one type of need for love.

The Hierarchy of Needs

The following information will help. It is a summary of the Hierarchy of Needs established by Abraham Maslow more than 50 years ago. The

Hierarchy implies that certain basic needs must be met before we are free to pursue the balance of our needs.

- **Level 1: Physiological:**
  food, air, water.
- **Level 2: Safety:**
  security, order, shelter, stability.
- **Level 3: Belonging and Love:**
  friendship, affectional relationships.
- **Level 4: Self-esteem:**
  self-respect, achievement, esteem of others.
- **Level 5: Self-actualization:**
  self-fulfillment, reaching your potential.

Physiological and safety needs are related to absolute survival. But the third tier represents the first human need: love. Because there are different kinds of love, it is important to recognize the different ways that love can be experienced.

Five Ways to Experience Love

- **Eros** creates union.
- **Filia** creates family-type love.
- **Agape** creates friendship.
- **Transpersonal** creates empathy for the human condition.
- **Divine** creates a sense of a higher power/creator/God/loving presence.

Even in a loving relationship, needs change. A relationship that commences in an Eros manner may evolve into a brother/sister relationship. One that begins as friends may become Eros. Even in an ongoing relationship, the dynamics of needs change. Sometimes the need is for a lover, sometimes a friend, sometimes an advisor, and sometimes the dominant need is for nurturing and comfort.

When one person's needs change and the other person is unable to accommodate the change, the relationship can suffer unless both parties' differing needs are addressed immediately. Relationships also suffer if one or both persons direct all of their needs into that one relationship. A single relationship can meet certain needs, but not all of them. It is each person's responsibility to know his/her needs and to create other relationships or interests to meet the needs that the primary relationship cannot meet.

Interpreting Our Needs

In the *Lifestyles of the Stressed and Strained* chapter, a Needs Exercise will help you and others begin to identify your needs. You can gain additional insights into your needs by paying attention to subconscious patterns: the ones that roam through your mind on a regular basis. In some instances these thoughts can be fantasies. You may think about winning the lottery and all the good things you would do for the world and for those you love. You may often think about starting your own business, being your own boss, and making more money with your creativity than your salaried job will ever allow. Continually planning trips to places you never actually go to, planning parties you never host, envisioning but never getting to the remodeling of your home... these are the types of thought patterns that reveal unmet needs.

Review the previous information on levels of needs and you may see a pattern. Security? Order? Esteem of others? Belonging? If you also take note of your thoughts throughout the day, you may see that you think about those activities or subjects because they reflect needs that your daily-life routine is not meeting. If so, you are expending a lot of time and energy in ways that do not meet some important needs. And that is compromising your relationship with love.

Knowing Our Children's Needs

Indigo Children can be intense, powerful Beings with intense, powerful needs. Their needs do not always complement their exceptional spiritual, intellectual, and creative gifts. Their needs can be so intense and demanding and complex that parents feel overwhelmed, and inadequate. If you are a parent or elder in one of these children's lives, consider and reflect on this information in your own behalf as well as your children's. The nature of needs is that they linger and often assert in subtle ways until they are met. When you (or your children) try to make changes, but witness yourself doing the familiar instead of the new, some need is at work underneath the familiar. Something about the familiar meets a powerful need.

This may apply to a simple-but-frustrating situation—like whatever causes us to continue accumulating unused items in the basement. Or the outcomes may be more self-defeating—like a series of speeding tickets. After reflecting on this information, and also benefiting from the Needs Exercise in *Lifestyles of the Stressed and Strained*, you will be better equipped to talk with your children about their needs, and work together on creating options that will meet their needs.

II. Anger: An Emotional Work-in-Progress

As a God-given emotion, anger has a purpose. Its purpose is to create change. The principal change anger produces is in relation to love: it challenges love to expand. It does so by challenging a situation that does not meet our needs and then enabling it to reorganize so it does. The result is love: our emotional response when our needs are met.

Anger is our emotional response when our needs are *not* met. Humanity's principal emotional need is for love. If the power of love within us has not created the circumstances we need, then our next emotional option is anger. Its extra-effort, purposefully disruptive energies are designed to challenge circumstances that do *not* meet our needs and rearrange those circumstances so they do.

In an ideal world, the power of the love within us would be sufficient to constantly create what we need. Or, the power of love within us would be sufficient to transform any anger that did arise. Then the supply of love within would enable us automatically to respond with patience, understanding, forgiveness, and compassion. Then anger would not be needed.

The Anger You Can Trust

Because anger is an emotion, managing it is an *emotional* responsibility. That is why these guidelines also teach how to experience more love. Love is the emotion that manages anger. The fact that anger and love are designed to co-exist is difficult for some people to trust. That is often because they associate anger with rage. Those individuals may have experienced rage in early life and they associate its properties with anger because anger is a more familiar term. That early-life association is also why some people are reluctant to admit or express their own anger. Their past conditioning causes them to equate anger as an unfair, unloving, untrustworthy emotion. Those are indeed the properties of emotional dysfunction because they accurately describe the condition of rage.

It is therefore important to remember that, unlike rage, anger is a proportional emotion. If we do not have a storehouse of built-up anger inside, enabling us to draw from it and overreact, then we can trust the amount of anger that comes up.

As a God-given emotion, anger is meted out in the quality and quantity of energy necessary to create the change that is needed. A minor offense may require only a raised voice. An intentional abuse will require a much more strident response. Because anger is designed to be non-enduring, however, once it is expressed, it has served its purpose and is replaced with the emotion that is enduring: love.

Anger is more intense than love, but love is more enduring. Anger is purposefully designed to be non-enduring so that, ideally, we do *not* suppress it and allow it to accumulate. The disturbing properties of anger that make it uncomfortable to hold on to are an incentive to express it at the time it wells up inside. That is when it has the potential to create change. Otherwise, if manipulated and suppressed, anger loses its creative properties and proportionality. That is when anger turns into rage.

We can trust our anger so long as we are in touch with love when we express it. That includes feeling self-love as well as love for the other person. As any parent knows, we can be very angry with a child and also very in touch with how much we love that young one. That is how children know they can trust our anger. They may not like our anger, but they can trust it if it is expressed with the presence of love. If we love our self as we express anger—love what we are saying, and how we are saying it—our anger can be trusted.

The Anger You Fear

Cumulative anger-based patterns produce distance or loss in connection with love. Healthy, loving people automatically protect themselves from the unpredictability and excess of suppressed anger once they have experience or witnessed it. They have to, for their own emotional well-being. They do not have a similar or matching reservoir inside, so they have no way to deflect or insulate from the potential emotional assaults.

Despite how nice, engaging, and well-meaning people with anger-based patterns may be at certain times, those who know the potential they have for "losing it" will not allow themselves to get close. Or, if they do get close and then experience or witness the abuse, they will create a protective barrier. At work, among friends, within the family, within one's self... there is no escape from the consequences of uncontrolled anger, the greatest of which is the loss of love.

If our own anger is out of control, we know it is driving love away. We may also by now be in touch with the particular fear that sets in. It is an added consequence of suppressed anger: the fear of not having enough love in our life. Sometimes this anger-related fear transfers to another aspect of our life, such as the fear of not having enough money. At its root, that fear is also connected to love, as the *Conditions of Emotional Dysfunction* chapter on these patterns outlines in more detail. That fear feels real. It can grip the subconscious in awful, tormenting ways. At those times, it is difficult to relate such fear to anger *or* to love. The fear simply seems consuming. If we experience any of these types of fears, our anger has not been used to ensure that our needs are met. Instead of challenging the love in our life to expand, our anger has accumulated for so long and to such a dysfunctional degree that it constantly restricts the experience of love in our life, including self-love. The more that love is compromised or lost (usually as a result of anger), the greater the fear.

Although fear is designed to engage temporarily when our life is in danger, if it accumulates as a result of anger, it is present constantly. That fear activates an alarm system inside. If the consequences of our anger have not yet motivated us to do something about it, this additional fear-related warning comes in. Unlike the anger, which is usually volatile on occasion but subsides at least *some* times, at this new level of cumulative emotional dysfunction, yet another signal is in place. This low-grade presence of fear lets us know that our connection to *love* is in danger.

III. What We Fear and Why

That's not the way fear is supposed to work. Its purpose is to let us know when our life is in danger. Its adrenaline-pumping energy is designed to course through the body and activate a self-protective action before our logical, rational mind has a chance to figure out a survival strategy. Because fear, like anger, is a proportional emotion, it makes certain its powerful energies are available for as long as necessary. Once the threat is passed, however, the fear dissipates to make way for the enduring emotion, love, to return.

Again like anger, fear is designed to be a non-enduring energy. It lasts only so long as there is a threat to life. The physical body is not equipped to continually stay on alert. Doing so not only uses up the body's resources and reserves. It also nullifies the automatic purpose and protection function of fear, because continuous anxiety keeps us from identifying and responding to "real" danger. The body stays engaged as though all moments are danger—which is precisely the dysfunction of anger-based fear. Our relationship with love is in danger, not our life, but the fear is engaged just the same.

Emotional Courage

If we recognize this development—the fear that our anger, expressed or suppressed, is jeopardizing our connection to love—it is important to summon the courage to express that fear. If we hold onto the fear because we're afraid to admit it or express it, and especially if we are afraid that expressing it will produce a loss of love, that is the very outcome we will create.

To dismantle this pattern, we must start by acknowledging our fear. If it is connected to a relationship, we can say something like: "I know you say you love me, but I am not feeling it. I am afraid you're going to find someone else more attractive, more intelligent, or more interesting." (Or, if your specific fear is different, acknowledge it and proceed. to add:) "What I need is for you to reassure me of your love. I also need us to find a way to manage the anger that erupts between us, because I am afraid it is going to destroy our love."

If instead the fear is related to losing your job, the same principle applies. You must act on it. Otherwise, the fear will preoccupy you emotionally and mentally, expand exponentially, and perhaps cause you to do something that actually does put your job at risk. In the workplace, therefore, your approach to fear can be simple, even businesslike.

If your workplace fear is nonspecific—nothing in particular has happened, but you have this generalized fear—you can say to your manager, "It's been a while since my last review, and I just wanted to confirm that my performance is meeting your standards." Or, if an actual incident is causing you to worry: "I realize my clash with the vice president created a strain between our two departments and I wanted to confirm that everything got resolved and my job is not at risk."

Summoning the emotional courage to act on the fear is an empowering experience. If the fear is unrealistic, acting on it not only alleviates the fear; it also expands our self-confidence and connects us with self-love. We love our self too much to continue living with this angst. If, on the other hand, the power of our self-love testing the fear does confirm the worst, at least we have not used up our emotional energy by an extended foray into the fear. We can harness that remaining emotional power and direct it into creativity, motivation, and self-assurance. That combination can help us recover from the unfulfilling relationship, or attract a new job. Experiencing the courage to express what we feel inevitably expands self-trust and self-love.

Emotional Truth

The first reason to express fear is to test whether it is realistic. Many fears that are based on the accumulation of anger are not realistic. An equally important reason to express fear is connected to emotional integrity. Hiding what we feel, and pretending we do not feel something when we do, are certain to erode self-trust and self-love. The very fact that anger has built up means we have not been truthful about the anger. The truth is, we got angry. The fact is, we denied or suppressed that anger. We pretended something was okay when it was not. "But I didn't want to hurt his feelings," we often say, when the truth is, "I didn't want to risk his anger." Or, the truth is, "I didn't love him enough to be truthful." Or, the truth is, "I didn't love myself enough to be truthful."

In those situations, by carefully twisting our thinking we can actually conclude that lying to someone won't hurt them; that it won't hurt their feelings if or when they do find out the truth. The only way we can possibly construct or defend that strategy is with suppressed anger. Love does not want to lie. Love does not need to lie. But love is compromised when we do lie. By manipulating our emotions and not being truthful about what we feel and need, we compromise our connection with love. When our life is not in danger but our connection with love is, the fear that results can be reduced through emotional courage and truth.

Emotional Healing

Acknowledging and releasing the fear enables the constant, cumulative anxiety to subside. Acknowledging the fear also keeps it from freezing the anger accumulated inside, which is the development that leads to the rage. Rage is not an emotion. It is a condition. As the chapter on *Conditions of Emotional Dysfunction* outlines, certain conditions develop when emotions are so shut down, so unavailable, and so chronically suppressed that they do not function. The energy from those suppressed emotions has to go somewhere, however, so over that long-term period of suppression, automatic patterns develop.

The most pernicious of those patterns results in rage: the uncontrolled, uncontrollable, destructive, and often deadly result of the extreme experience of UnLove. Wholly lacking a connection with love, its most significant characteristic is the lack of emotional conscience. As the product of ancient anger frozen in place, rage is removed from the creative properties of love, from the potential for change through anger, and from the life-saving function of fear.

As the principles and guidelines in this book suggest, however, there are ways to reverse the rage. And once a person makes the changes that reinstate the experience of love, that internal inferno of rage can subside. Then the love within enables the person to manage and express the anger so it does not continue to accumulate into rage.

Children's Rage

Children's rage is not about what they have done to compromise love; it is about the lack or loss of love. A child's rage is an indication of how powerless that child feels in connection with experiencing adequate love. That does not necessarily mean the child is in an unloving environment. A child can be in a loving environment but not *experience* the love. That is the nature of patterns. They restrict the experience of love. However, the principles for reversing rage contained in this book give children and others the opportunity to reconnect with love. The *Conditions of Emotional Dysfunction* and *Return to Love* chapters describe how releasing the sadness commences that reversal and creates powerful new possibilities for experiencing love.

Fear and Rage

Until that change, however, rage can be a constantly threatening, negative state. The cumulative patterns creating the rage originally formed for a purpose. Some emotional event or environment felt unsafe or unloving, and the patterns formed to insulate the vulnerable individual (usually a tiny child) from the pain of that reality. The patterns, therefore, have a consciousness. They were formed to protect, and they continue to gird themselves to do so.

The consciousness of rage is no exception. Its function is to protect from the sadness of UnLove and it does so, literally, with a vengeance. The negative state of rage is constant. According to its consciousness, it must be. To preserve itself, rage must therefore control and be in control, especially in relation to emotional reality. Rage therefore imagines, recalls, and relentlessly replays events in the same way so it can continue blaming the same people and the same situations. In doing so, rage not only successfully functions as a defense from the truth; it is also a defense from the extreme pain and fear of UnLove.

Because rage is the result of both anger- and fear-based patterns fused together, the steps to dismantling rage must address both. The anger underneath rage is related to the extreme experience of feeling unloved. The fear of re-experiencing that deep pain is so great that even though the person realizes the rage drives love away, it also serves as insulation. In fact, the extent of a person's rage is a measure of the emotional protection required to avoid the anticipated pain of UnLove.

This usually means that early in life the person experienced someone else's rage: someone's anger that had built up to such a degree that when it was unleashed, it was unloving, unfair, judgmental, and punishing. To survive such an environment, the child's own rage increased, both because the raging circumstances were so extremely unloving, and also because the child's cumulative rage was needed as protection. The rage kept an emotionally sensitive child from staying open to such circumstances and being emotionally devoured.

Even if the person is in a loving environment, the rage is still an indication of the pain of living without adequate love. This is often the situation in relationships. Two people can bring love to the relationship, but rage from the past can be a recurring threat to fulfillment and stability.

The person who reaches adulthood with rage-based patterns inside is also emotionally frozen in fear. The fear is that dismantling that rage and admitting the truth of the fear of UnLove will be equally punitive and painful. As the rage discussions in this book explain, however, there are ways to defuse that condition, starting with the human emotion that accumulates after the rage has taken its toll: sadness.

IV. The Message of Sadness

Underneath the long-term unmet need for love lies a deep pocket of sadness. Originating early in life in response to longing for but not experiencing adequate love, the sadness has continued to accumulate in adolescence and adulthood every time the rage destroyed love or the fear blocked it. Like the other three basic emotions, sadness serves a purpose. It is our emotional response to the loss of love. At the same time, it too has a function. The function of sadness is to expand our emotional capacity so that after the sadness is experienced and released, and after we learn its message about love, we then have a greater capacity to experience and attract love. The *Return to Love* chapter outlines this process in greater detail.

The Lesson Is Love

Part of that greater capacity to experience love comes from the insights about love obtained when we release the sadness. Accordingly, sadness teaches us about love. It has been our automatic emotional response every time we experienced loss of love. Within the sadness there is, therefore, a memory of everything we said or did that distanced or compromised that love.

As we experience and release the sadness, we see the patterns we repeated that have resulted in the accumulation of sadness. If we had been sufficiently emotionally adequate to experience and express the sadness at the time we experienced the loss or lack of love, the sadness would not have accumulated. The fact that it is stored within, however, indicates we did not have that emotional adequacy or maturity at the time.

Releasing the sadness reveals the lessons about love. How we compromised it, mistrusted it, denied, resented, and betrayed it. We see what we did and why. What we could now change and how. We see the previous needs, the lack of emotional courage, and often, the similarity between patterns in our childhood and those we have enacted that have kept us from love. These and other insights produced from releasing the sadness become the guidelines for helping us return to love. If we could have experienced and released the sadness at the time it arose, we could have heeded its message and perhaps not repeated the actions that had distanced us from love. Instead, continuing to accumulate the sadness inside has distanced us even further from love.

Until we release the sadness, we do not gain insight into the destructive patterns that produce the loss of love. And until we change those patterns, we will not attract the quality and quantity of love in our life that we need.

The Teacher Is Sadness

To dissolve the patterns that have distanced us from love, we must acknowledge the truth of those patterns. We must also acknowledge the toll they will continually take on our emotional well-being. That means we must not only experience the release of the accumulated sadness. We must also face the rage and the accumulated fears, and then learn how to express anger in a manner that does not destroy the connection to love.

"But how can I release the sadness?" you might ask. And the answer is, we do not have to focus on releasing it. Once we stop suppressing the sadness, it will emerge with the message about being and behaving in a manner that reclaims our relationship with love. For the sadness to emerge, and also to release other emotions that have been subject to suppression, it will help to start paying attention to what we are feeling at all times. The nature of suppression is that the mind fixates on familiar thought patterns, reviewing the same events and fantasies over and over again, ensuring that such mental exercises are so encompassing that they override the underlying emotions.

As we begin to pay closer attention, we will recognize those familiar thoughts that regularly roam through our subconscious. That is our cue to ask, "What am I feeling right now?" After practicing this a few times, we will realize there are feelings underneath those thoughts. If we cannot identify anger or fear as the underlying emotion, it is most likely sadness. Reflecting on those thought patterns more closely will put us in touch with the sadness. Allowing our self to experience the sadness and release it will reveal the changes for us to make to reconnect with love.

The defense mechanism that originally engaged to suppress our sadness is understandable. When the sadness first accumulated in connection with inadequate love, it felt unbearable to us as a little child. So we exiled that sadness into the body and stored with a memory that to ever experience the sadness again would be equally unbearable. As our adult self has emotionally matured, however, we have a greater capacity to feel and release the sadness. Admittedly, doing so requires emotional courage and trust. But the risk of holding it inside is indeed much greater, and certainly much more painful, than releasing it and discovering the pathway back to love.

Notes

Chapter Five

Identifying the
Hidden Symptoms of Anger™

But How Do You Know You're Angry?

You can have fun getting to know this information! You also can find it extremely useful and reliable in tracking indicators of anger that has been suppressed. The information in this chapter has been compiled and verified for more than 20 years. Some of it may be familiar to you. If you are unfamiliar with the specifics of anger-related symbology, however, some of this information may be completely new to you.

New information is constantly available these days to help us better understand ourselves and the situations in our daily lives. If these anger-related indicators differ from other interpretive information you've encountered and relied on, that is because information available to our consciousness hundreds, even thousands of years ago, does continue to expand.

Body, mind, and spirit have evolved. When you attracted to you certain information in the past, that information was undoubtedly what you needed at that time. Now that you are learning about anger, this body of information is likely to be useful to you. If for some reason you try out this information and do not find it credible, trust yourself. These indicators are supplemental; they are offered to help you identify certain *subtleties* of anger. The bigger value of this book is contained in the details for transforming the anger you already know is a problem!

The Love/Anger Contrast

The first time you look at some of the entries on this list, you may wonder how they could possibly be connected to anger. They are *not* the product of anger that is expressed in a spontaneous, self-loving manner. These are the outcomes of anger that has been denied, withheld, suppressed, and manipulated. For those reasons, the anger is "hidden."

To better understand the meaning of each of these entries, keep in mind:

- **Love** is the emotion that facilitates.
- **Anger** is the emotion that obstructs.
- **Love** is the emotion of balance.
- **Anger** is the emotion of excess.

As you consider this Love/Anger contrast, together with the principles contained throughout this book, you will see more clearly how these indicators reveal a hidden connection with anger.

Built-up anger reduces a person's emotional security. That person may then compensate, over-do, try too hard, and need too much. The outcome of such efforts is unfulfilling and self-defeating. Others sense the underlying emotional need or inadequacy and react to it, sometimes knowingly, and at other times, simply automatically. That's why efforts like people-pleasing are anger-based.

Without sufficient self-love inside, the person tries to obtain a sense of value or closeness by, for example, meeting others' needs. That strategy may not *obviously* be connected to anger, because pleasing would appear to be more an act of love rather than need. It is anger-related, however, when it is done from a hidden agenda or motive. Anger tends to hide, deny, cover up, and rationalize. Love wants everything disclosed and out in the open. Love seeks and is secure with the truth.

Timing Is Everything

What makes this interpretive information helpful and illuminating is that it coincides with whatever subconscious or unconscious pattern is present in your mind that produces these symptoms. Pay attention, therefore, to what you were thinking or saying or hearing or experiencing when you notice one of these symptoms... such as when you sneeze. Sneezes signify anger. They are a mild form of indicating that you do not like what you just heard or thought. Someone else's sneezes mean the same thing. That person does not like what he/she just heard or was thinking or experiencing.

The supplemental text offered with certain entries in this chapter will expand your understanding and application of these "messages from down under"—these Hidden Symptoms of Anger™ stored in the body that make the subtle presence of anger known.

Once you know the messages, and take note of the instant they appear, that information will help you identify and modify certain indicators of anger in your own emotional and physical being.

The Hidden Symptoms of Anger™

- Addictions
- Clutter
- Parking tickets
- Excessive giving
- Neglect
- Complaining
- Nail biting
- Speeding
- Lying
- Bounced checks
- Twisted phone cords
- Tangled appliance cords
- Excessive talking
- Secrets
- Being overprotective
- Depression
- Invading someone's space—physical *and* emotional
- Resentment
- Enabling
- Under-tipping servers, valets, haircutters, etc.
- Excessive time on the phone

- Control vs. motivation
- Stealing
- Gossiping
- Eating fast
- Not paying bills
- Snooping
- Unrealistic expectations
- Frequent job changes
- Dwelling on the past
- Unsustainable relationships
- Excessive Internet use
- Mistreating animals
- Exploiting
- Excessive spending
- Teasing
- Scratching your nose
- Withholding information
- Abuse
- Intimidation
- Not returning phone calls
- Blaming
- Chronically being late
- Chronically forgetting
- Ignoring
- Using guilt to obtain an outcome
- Playing violent computer or video games
- Watching violent movies
- Asking excessive questions
- Shaming
- Procrastination
- Stacks of newspapers or unread mail
- Tailgating
- Frequently interrupting
- Losing or misplacing things
- Excessive drinking
- Hostility

- Stereotyping
- Demanding
- Inability to share
- Promising more than you can deliver
- Judging
- Hidden agendas
- Not returning borrowed items
- Exaggerating
- Asking people to repeat what they said
- Dependency
- Sarcasm
- Not keeping commitments
- Dishonesty
- Aggressive personality
- People-pleasing
- Manipulation
- Impatience
- Consistently speaking too loudly
- Denial
- Excessive eating
- Seduction
- Hitting "in fun"
- Prejudice
- Not repairing items
- Excessive accumulation in car, basement, garage, etc.
- Burned food
- "Accidents"
- Scratches
- Inflammation
- Fever
- Sneezes
- Allergies
- Off-color jokes
- Talking "behind another's back"
- Body piercing
- Not paying taxes

- Illegally copying software, music, movies, etc.
- Jealousy
- Cheating
- Needing to be "right"
- Saying it doesn't matter when it does
- Greed
- Running out of gas
- Employing humor as an anger cover-up
- Seeking security through hidden vs. open disclosure and communication

Now that you know what to look for, you may even add your own indicators to the list. Ideally, this information will continue to speak to you and add to your own capacity to identify anger and anger-related patterns that may be compromising your relationship with love.

Chapter Six

Conditions of Emotional Dysfunction

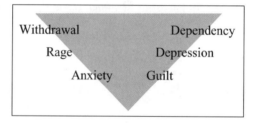

Withdrawal		Dependency
Rage		Depression
	Anxiety	Guilt

Introduction

Throughout this book, there are many examples of the consequences of suppressing emotions. The Symbology chapter describes how suppressed emotions affect our physical body. This chapter is devoted to discussing the effects of suppression on the emotional body.

When children are not able to express their emotions, either because drugs restrict expression or patterns deny expression, the conditions described in this chapter develop. These same conditions often remain through adolescence and into adulthood. This topic is presented so parents and teachers can understand these conditions in Indigo Children of all ages. In addition, this information will enable parents, teachers, and other elders to gain insight into the developmental process that produces these conditions, and to help children reverse the conditions.

The other benefit of this information is *for* parents, teachers, and other elders. Because of the transgenerational potential for these conditions to be passed from elders to children, this information assists everyone in applying the principles for transforming these conditions into emotional well-being.

The conditions discussed in this chapter are anger-based. They specifically relate to anger that is suppressed because of unmet needs for love from others. Accordingly, this chapter offers a unique perspective for understanding the terms and developmental process associated with conditions of emotional dysfunction that originate with suppressing anger. Familiar terms like "anxiety" and "withdrawal" are discussed in a specific context: as consequences that develop from originally suppressing anger.

In keeping with the principles of Transforming Anger Into Love™, these conditions are examined in connection with the four basic human emotions: love, anger, fear, and sadness. When we *sup*press rather than *ex*press any of these emotions, the energy of the emotion eventually accumulates into patterns. In addition, because the suppression becomes automatic, the patterns that develop become automatic. Although one of the emotions may be activated, it is rerouted into the automatic patterns rather than being spontaneously, dynamically expressed.

These suppression-related developments as described in this chapter lead to conditions of emotional dysfunction. This descriptive term applies to (1) suppressed (2) automatic (3) unloving (4) patterns. Under these conditions, the basic emotional impulse connected to love, anger, fear, or sadness is not acknowledged. It is therefore not trusted and not integrated. Instead, the activated emotion is manipulated (*i.e.*, suppressed).

When the emotion is automatically manipulated rather than expressed, the quantity of suppressed emotional energy becomes overwhelming, and the pattern of suppression becomes overwhelmingly powerful. At that point, this suppression mechanism displaces the option of a spontaneous expression of the emotion. Any emotion so constantly suppressed lingers below the surface and steadily accumulates. *On* the surface, meanwhile, the cumulative outcome manifests as a condition.

Conditions and Emotions

Being activated but consistently denied expression causes an emotion eventually to default into a **condition**: a non-dynamic, unproductive, dysfunctional state. Since that emotional energy is then essentially unavailable, the resulting condition dilutes our emotional power and security as well as our emotional integrity and maturity.[1]

Inevitably, then, because the condition originates due to suppressed anger, it compromises our relationship with love. A variety of consequences can occur. Many of those consequences are set forth in three particular chapters in this book: *Identifying Hidden Symptoms of Anger*, in *Emotions, Energy and the Body: A Guide to Symbology, Meaning and Understanding*, and in *Transforming Anger Into Love™*.

None of the consequences of suppressing emotions is more dramatic than the extreme, emotionally dysfunctional condition of rage. Many Indigo Children have experienced rage. Before the consequences of suppressing emotions reach that extreme, however, the suppressed emotions progress through stages. At any one of the stages, we can help these children. If we can identify the *patterns* that are developing, we can help children avoid the *conditions*. And, if we recognize the *conditions*, we can help children transform the patterns that sustain them.

As anyone who is the parent, teacher, mentor, or friend of an Indigo Child knows, these children can be acutely sensitive. They often have feelings of not belonging. They often feel misunderstood. In addition, they often are labeled: "problem kids," "learning disabled," "Attention Deficit Disorder," or "Attention Deficit Hyperactive Disorder." As a result, their emotional and intellectual needs are often misunderstood and misdiagnosed.

If the sensitivity of Indigo Children is not honored, and their emotional

---

[1] Throughout this book, emotional integrity means expressing the truth of what we feel at the time we feel it. That is contrasted to the inclination to deny or suppress feelings and thereby not be accountable for the truth of those feelings. Likewise, throughout this book, the term emotional maturity means that, in accordance with emotional integrity, emotions have not been suppressed. They have been present, accounted for, and integrated in the physical, mental, and psychological maturing process.

needs are not met, they often suppress those aspects of themselves. The sadness associated with not belonging, the anger at being continually misjudged and misunderstood, the fear of not meeting others' expectations... if these accumulate within children, the conditions described in this chapter can develop. Add Ritalin and its counterparts to the mix, thereby imposing yet another layer of suppression (this time, behavior), and it is understandable that these children become anxious or depressed. It is no wonder they scream with rage, feel guilty and frustrated because they can't "get it right," or sink into withdrawal because of feeling, "What's the use?"

Whether the consequence is withdrawal, anxiety, depression, or any of the other conditions described herein, the originating emotion is anger and the principal emotion compromised is love. Originally, anger is a message about our *need* for love. But if anger is not expressed, it accumulates in a manner that obstructs our *capacity* to feel love.

Dependency is the condition that first obstructs our relationship with love. Since all of the conditions are a symptom of not experiencing adequate love, if we are able to avoid the condition of dependency, we can avoid the other conditions. For that reason, much of this chapter addresses dependency. It does so in a manner that elders can relate to, and thereby transfer the information and principles to their young children's lives.

Dependency and Love

About Dependency: The Condition

Dependency is the condition that results when the dynamic, expansive flow of love has been restricted by the accumulation of unexpressed anger. Anger is our emotional response when our needs are not met. Our principal emotional need is for love. If anger arises within us and is not expressed, unless it is transformed by the love within us, it accumulates inside.[2] If anger accumulates, our needs are not being met.

Since love is our emotional response when our needs *are* met, if we remain in such an environment—wherein our needs are not being met, and we continue to suppress our anger—the dynamic emotion in such a situation is not love. It is anger, suppressed and denied. As elders, many of us have experienced this at some time in our lives. When the love shuts down but we stay in a relationship anyway, the overriding condition holding us there is dependency. The same is true in a job situation. If the value we need to feel shuts down, perhaps because we are not paid what we are worth or the company does not keep its word, and we are angry but we stay at the job anyway, a dependent situation is set up.

Occasionally, there is sufficient respect and maturity in a relationship to create a healthy way to stay together under these circumstances, perhaps for the children or the family-run business. Or, if we make a mature, self-loving decision to stay at the job and are able to avoid the constant turbulence of pent-up anger, that, too, can be a healthy choice. But usually, such decisions are based on the condition of dependency. In that case, the anger is not transformed, it does smolder below the surface, and we do remain locked into a limiting, unfulfilling situation. Those outcomes are the result of continuing to deny our anger, thereby abridging its capacity/purpose to create change.

These dependent dynamics have usually been perpetuated over and over in our lives because we do not know how to attract a relationship or situation that is adequate to meet our needs. Underneath this pattern is a truth: we do not know what our needs are, nor do we know how to inventory a relationship or situation to determine whether it has the capacity to meet our needs. Under these circumstances, our need for love has never adequately been met, which means that our need for love is increasingly intense. To the degree we remain in a relationship or situation that does not meet our needs, our anger also becomes increasingly intense.

We allow these inadequate situations to continue because our inner emotional security is not sufficiently strong to enable us to leave. We are unable to access the self-love to make a self-loving change. Our compromised emotional power and security often compromise our financial power and security, as well. So we remain, dependent on someone else

---

[2] As the principles for Transforming Anger Into Love™ throughout this book state, love is the emotion that manages anger. If we have sufficient love within, then even in a situation that does not meet our needs, we are able to respond with love-based options instead of anger. Those options include patience, understanding, compassion, and forgiveness. The difference between those responses and simply not expressing our anger—(suppressing it instead, while we "act" patient or forgiving)—is that the love within us completely absorbs the anger that arises, and we never think about the situation again. Suppressed anger, however, lingers beneath the surface and continually reminds us of the event and of the anger we still harbor. Rather than being absorbed, the anger has been denied.

because we have forfeited our emotional power by denying the truth of our needs and our anger.

Arrangements to stay together under these terms are frequently described as angry/dependent. Anger is the emotional dynamic that holds them together, and the anger is in response to unmet needs. Contrary to continuing in a relationship because it meets our needs, we stay in one that doesn't. Contrary to experiencing more love as a result of our needs being met, we experience more and more anger. This is part of the emotional dysfunction.

Because this pattern is familiar, we know how to navigate it. Despite its inevitable outcome, we know the nuances of each developmental stage. We have survived each stage in the past and we are confident we can do so again. In the meantime, we use our suppressed anger as a constant, protective semblance of emotional power. If we had expressed our anger at the time we felt it, the anger could have been utilized to challenge the love in the relationship, or the self-love within us, to expand. When the anger within us expands instead, it eventually stops the dynamic flow of love.

This is the development that seals the dependent condition in place. It is the result when the dynamic, expansive flow of love has been restricted by the accumulation of unexpressed anger. This development is part of a pattern, it is familiar, we know how to navigate it, and we've survived it many times before. The pattern most likely, then, started in early life. That is why this information is included in this book.

These developments may be underway in your own family, and the easiest way to recognize them in others is to review them in connection to ourselves. If we have perpetuated this pattern as elders, we learned it for survival in early-life. In some manner, not all of our early-life needs for love were met.[3] We were angry as a result, and we were certainly dependent as a little child. So we developed a pattern or two to enable us to remain in that situation without expressing our anger.

(It is possible our children have adopted some of these same patterns. It is possible some of these dynamics are connected to the anger that

---

[3] It is unintended that all our needs be met in our early-life environment. If that environment had met all our needs, we would still be there! Instead, those unmet needs carry forth in life and are met by friends, teachers, mentors, colleagues, business partners, and intimate partners.

Indigo Children and families experience.)

As elders in the throes of relationship dynamics, we often are unwilling to express our needs and our anger for fear they will put the relationship at risk. This is the first indicator that the relationship already *is* at risk because of its innate inadequacy. If we do not express the truth of what we feel and what we need at the time our feelings and needs arise, it is usually in denial of the truth we are already recognizing. Although our dependency keeps us from acting on the truth, the truth always, eventually, will prevail. Furthermore, because we have enacted this pattern over and over again, we know by now that a situation that is inadequate ultimately cannot be sustained.

Only the angry, dependent condition that is continually gathering momentum is sufficiently powerful to deny that ever-present truth. And indeed, that is the function of the dependency. It denies the presence of anger, and, therefore, the inadequacy of the love available in the situation.

(The chapters on *Identifying Hidden Symptoms of Anger* and *The Hidden Power of Love* offer helpful guidelines for distinguishing between loving, adequate situations, and angry, dependent ones. In addition, the Needs Exercise in the chapter *Lifestyles of the Stressed and Strained* will help identify needs in behalf of parents, children, and the entire family.)

About Love: The Emotion

When two people bring love to a relationship, the only possible outcome is more love. When two people *need* love and pretend they have it to give, saying, "I love you," actually means, "I need you." Saying, "I love you," *implies*, "I have love to give." However, the truth in a dependent condition is: "I *need* love, and even though this relationship is inadequate, and I know it won't last, I can't bear to be alone, so I'll deny my own needs, and try to meet your needs, so I can stay in this situation.

"To do so, I will deny the truth and the inadequacies of the situation and I will hold my anger inside. It signifies the truth of my unmet needs, and I am not able to face that truth. I will, instead, bury myself in the dynamics of dysfunction, again, until the bitter end."

Anger is the test in an adequate relationship. When self-love is present, we do not fear expressing anger. In fact, the integrity of love ensures that we express our anger. Love derives its security from truth and honesty.

Self-love expands in the expression of truth and honesty. Love also knows that being untruthful about anger is sure to allow that nettlesome emotion to accumulate and obstruct the love. In addition, love is so secure that it knows it can survive the intensity of anger. Love has no reason to avoid or not express anger. Love knows anger creates change. Love knows anger challenges situations and brings forth even greater potential to experience love. Love is secure in that dynamic because love knows it is adequate.

If needs arise in our partner, family, or job situation, and we cannot personally meet those needs, the love within us is sufficiently secure to acknowledge that truth. Love knows its value. Love knows its worth. Love also knows its limitations and does not feel insecure in the truth of them. Love knows it is adequate and knows it is not required to over-compensate or over-extend in order to sustain a balanced, equitable relationship or situation.

Dependency does not have that security within. It derives its security from meeting others' needs. In so doing, it forfeits its own needs. That is how the anger accumulates. Eventually, the anger from unmet needs is so great, and the supply of love is so inadequate, that the condition that shuts down love develops into depression: the condition that shuts down anger.

Depression and Anger

Depression is a condition, not a feeling. It is an awful condition, in fact, that results in a serious and often debilitating emotional shutdown. While that shutdown dramatically restricts the experience and expression of love, including self-love, the emotion that depression directly shuts down is anger. That outcome is the result of suppression so cumulative and severe that the anger loses its emotional power and purpose and defaults into the non-dynamic, consuming condition of depression.

Life is difficult even when we have sufficient love in our lives. But at least with the dynamic of love flowing in and around us, we have hope and we experience moments of real joy and pleasure. We retain connection with people and activities that are meaningful. We are able to remind ourselves of the blessings and possibilities obtainable in our lives, even in periods when those may not be abundant.

Depression can be so enveloping that it blots out all of those hopeful thoughts and options. In a depressed state, we see the negative. We expect the negative. What we talk about is negative. And in this self-destructive condition, we manage to produce one negative outcome after the other. Depression is, therefore, a testament to the relentless power of accumulated anger. It requires immediate emotional attention when either we or our children sink into its abyss.

Because this dysfunctional condition keeps us from feeling or expressing anger in a spontaneous, productive manner, our anger remains trapped below the surface. It is seldom acknowledged because in this condition, we do not *feel* the anger when it is activated. Instead, the well-developed suppression patterns ensure that our spontaneous anger is suppressed and exiled into a reservoir of old, negative emotional power.

At least in the dependency condition discussed earlier, we feel the anger. We do not express it for fear it will drive away love, but that is a calculated choice. At that beginning stage of emotional dysfunction, we do feel the spikes of anger. We simply suppress them for as long as possible, deluding ourselves that to do so will sustain a loving relationship. When suppressing the anger instead shuts down the dynamic flow of love, and yet we remain in such an unfulfilling situation, it is the result of dependency. Anger flourishes in that environment. It is not spontaneous, healthy, change-producing anger. It is passive/aggressive, uncontrolled, or a love/hate kind of anger. In a dependent condition, the anger is dynamic and cumulative. The problem is, the *love* is not.

With depression, neither the love *nor* the anger is dynamic. Originally designed as an automatic response when our needs (for love) are not met, the anger has been relentlessly manipulated, in denial of its message. In these circumstances, our anger has continually confirmed the truth. "This situation is not adequate. I am not experiencing the love I need." However, in an effort to preserve these (inadequate) situations, we continually suppress the anger and its God-given function, which is to challenge love to expand. Eventually, then, the anger succumbs. The numbing pattern of suppression wins. The anger is no longer engagable as a tool to expand love. It is no longer employed as an emotion to produce change. As a result, the anger defaults into depression: the condition that immobilizes our capacity to experience and express anger in a spontaneous, healthy manner.

Love Experienced Is Love Expressed

While these progressive dynamics and outcomes of depression can be detected, other symptoms can be more subtle, particularly in children. Accordingly, it helps to remember that love experienced is love expressed. A child who is experiencing love will express love. This applies even to adolescents who are developing personalities and exploring new emotional dynamics and defenses. If they are experiencing love, that will show through a certain familiar loving look in their eyes; a spontaneous, loving gesture; a thoughtful observation or communication. These and similar indicators of love will always manifest, even during the most intense emotional rites of passage and awkward stages of emotional development and maturation.

Our children's healthy anger will show, as well. We may find their anger and attitudes quite unappealing at times; but anger is an ordinary, even appropriate, response to certain stresses in daily life. Their anger is a message about needs. Their needs are a way to experience love. It is healthy if children express their anger at the moment they feel it, do not hold it inside, and do not allow it to accumulate out of proportion and out of control. If children's anger accumulates to the degree that it displaces their relationship with love, that is a warning sign. If we notice children's expression of anger diminish, or if their emotional affect becomes significantly less expressive, these are indicators that their anger may be turning inward. In that instance, the patterns that develop into depression may be underway.

Seeking competent, compassionate professional assistance is always a good idea for any situation that restricts our emotional well-being. This is especially true with depression, whether our own or our children's. As the inspiring interview with homeopath and therapist Melanie Melvin, Ph.D., indicates, homeopathy can be extremely effective in helping with the underlying factors that contribute to depression. In addition, there are principles suggested throughout this book to assist in reversing the types of unproductive patterns that perpetuate anger and compromise love. As the information in *Transforming Anger Into Love*™ suggests, the principles for addressing anger start with recognizing and valuing our needs because, when they are met, needs enable us to experience more love.

Love is the emotion that manages anger. Depression is a condition resulting from a serious buildup of anger that blocks us from experiencing love. From the emotional perspective, increasing our experience of love, as well as increasing our supply of self-love within, adds to our emotional potential for transforming anger, even if the anger is buried in depression.

In the model for Transforming Anger Into Love™, a dual approach is utilized for addressing depression: The Anger/Love Axis™. Unless our automatic patterns of suppressing anger are dismantled, the patterns producing depression cannot be reversed. But we must also find a way to increase our experience of love, and to add to the supply of love within, we must start with our needs. Meeting our needs will enable us to experience more love.

In cases of serious depression, we may have lost touch with our needs. If the depression has consumed us for a long time, it may have been a long time since we experienced the joy of some one or some thing meeting our needs. If you or someone you know is in this condition, the following exercise can help. It begins with thinking back through certain times and activities you have enjoyed throughout your life and, with pen and paper, creating a log of those activities.

Maybe you remember enjoying fishing when you were in junior high. Even though that might not appeal to you now, you can recall which aspects of that activity did appeal to you then. Now you write them down. Chances are, the enjoyment was not simply standing on the bank of a lake, tossing filament and a baited hook into the water, and waiting, and waiting, for a fish to bite. Perhaps you enjoyed the time alone with a parent or favorite relative or friend. Although that person may not be available in your life right now, continue the exercise of remembering the times and the activities you enjoyed, and why, and write them down.

In the fishing example, part of the fun may have been accumulating and selecting favorite lures, a hobby that might not fit your lifestyle at this time. It is good to remember those times, however, and which aspects were fulfilling, so continue with this exercise. Recall and write down all the exchanges and activities that you enjoyed, and why. Maybe in the fishing example, you enjoyed being out of doors. Maybe it's been a long time since you sat in the park or paid attention to the sky or listened to the birds. Maybe you haven't noticed the flower gardens and landscaping in your neighborhood or throughout your city. As you recall and log the good memories, make an effort to *emotionally* reconnect with the activities you enjoyed. Then you can think about choices available in your life now that can bring similar enjoyment and meaning.

In order to experience more love, you must start with self-love. It is the only love you can actually create. And, when you have love inside, you automatically attract more. You also are able to be more creative when you have more love within because love is the creative emotion. With additional love inside, you can mobilize your self to create some options in your life that will rekindle the meaning and joy in your life.

In all efforts to reverse these powerful conditions, it is important to start small. Avoid focusing on how far you have regressed. Avoid focusing on how much effort it will take to reclaim your old self. If depression drags you into such negative, self-defeating thoughts, re-focus on the good times this exercise is designed to help you recall. Practice maintaining your focus on those moments in the past that brought you joy. This will help fortify you to make changes you have lacked the emotional power or motivation to create within your self and your life.

Anger Expressed is Depression Displaced

Identifying our needs can be difficult when we are depressed. That is why the previous simple exercise can be so helpful. Instead of requiring us to imagine what would meet our needs right now, it focuses our emotional attention on experiences we can recall. Once we recall the experiences and write down what we enjoyed about them, we have a list available to guide us into activities we can pursue in the present. Then the challenge is to follow through with the list.

To create the space within us to allow new, positive experiences, it helps to address the unproductive accumulations in our environment. When depression has displaced love, our spectrum of life experiences narrows dramatically. Letting certain self-care duties slide is a good example. Witnessing this deterioration in our circumstances can even compound the depression.

The laundry piles up, the cupboards are bare, the house is a mess, and the oil change is postponed again. Every time we promise to get to those things and depression intervenes, we feel even worse. When things are this overwhelming, we may need some outside help from friends or from people whose businesses provide such services. If our budget allows, we might bring in a housecleaning service just to get our lives back to scratch. We might also consider having our clothes laundered. Acting on self-care messages and insights will help immensely in regaining a sense of power and self-worth. Depression does not completely block the messages; it blocks our capacity to act on them. If we summon the emotional energy to reinstate something we enjoy, we have accessed the self-love that can continue to expand. Then we can add yet another meaningful action, and remove yet another symbol of neglect.

These accomplishments replenish our sense of value and hope, and eventually we will gather the emotional energy to identify or act on whatever is causing our anger. It *is* the emotion underlying the depression, and it is also the emotion sufficiently dynamic and powerful to dismantle the depression.

Anger is basically a message about love. Depression is basically the experience of not feeling love. Underneath each of the conditions discussed in this chapter there is an emotion that has been manipulated (suppressed). In the development of depression, that emotion is anger. It is the emotion that produces change. If we can add to the supply of love within, that will give us additional emotional energy to harness our internalized anger. The anger can then be directed toward changing those patterns we are perpetuating in our lives that keep us from feeling adequate love.

Another written exercise may help us focus on the anger we have lost touch with. In this instance, it helps once again to think back to the past because depression is a long-term buildup of unexpressed anger. It may have been a while since we spontaneously used our anger to create the changes we needed. In this exercise, we begin with current circumstances and think backward. We look for the last time we expressed our anger. We write that down. What was our need at that time? We write that, too. Did our anger help us obtain the change we needed? If so, how? If not, why not? Perhaps the reason is that we waited so long and allowed our anger to build to such a degree that when we expressed it, it was too late, or too much.

So we keep thinking and reviewing and logging these recollections. We think further about when we expressed anger; what our need was; how our anger worked to create the change we needed; or how our anger did not work, and why. As we review both our anger and our needs, we gain insight into the anger-based patterns that have accumulated. We then can begin to see what patterns we are allowing now that are not meeting our needs. Some of these patterns are causing us to feel angry, but we are not expressing the anger. As we continue this exercise, we will identify several situations in which we can begin to consciously direct our anger in a manner that will create change. We can see the patterns and *feel* our anger. Activating this anger will help dislodge it from the depressive state. Mobilizing the anger will give us emotional power to create the changes we need.

This retrospective exercise will not change our suppressive patterns overnight. But it will at least reclaim our connection with our anger, and help to diminish the power of the patterns and conditions that suppressing our anger perpetuates. Then we can apply the principles for *reporting* our anger, as described in the following topic of *Guilt and the Anger/Fear Connection*.

In combination, changing the supply of love and reconnecting with our needs and anger can contribute significantly to breaking up the patterns perpetuating the depression. This process may feel difficult when viewed through the lens of depression. However, it can be very, very effective, so somehow, find a way to get underway. Then several things will start to improve. These exercises are not intended to be a substitute for the professional help that depression deserves. They can, however, be a useful complement to the guidance from a mental health professional.

Even if we start small—like, taking out a stack of newspapers, taking a short walk, or making a grocery list that includes two of our favorite foods—we have at least begun the process of change. The progress will feel good. It will begin adding back to our sense of power and self-worth. Gradually, we will regain sufficient connection with self-love to effectively redirect and utilize our anger. It is the underlying suppressed emotion that contributes to depression. It is also the undeniable emotional option for breaking through depression and experiencing love.

Guilt and the Anger/Fear Connection

Guilt is the condition that results from the combination of suppressed anger and suppressed fear. If we feel guilty about something, we have both anger and fear but we are not expressing either one. We remain angry about something that occurred in the past. We also fear the consequences in the future if we express our anger. Because we don't express either emotion, they both remain suppressed, and they develop into the non-dynamic condition of guilt.

As the anger-based conditions outlined in this chapter develop, they take a progressive toll on our emotional vitality. This is true of dependency. It certainly is true of depression. And it also applies to the condition of guilt. Guilt is purposefully designed to make us so uncomfortable that we rid ourselves of it. The longer we distance ourselves from the truth of what we feel, the greater the degree of discomfort. The sooner we tell the truth, the sooner we are free of the guilt. Since emotional well-being starts with emotional integrity, ridding ourselves of guilt not only removes an emotional burden, it also brings life back to our emotions.

In all the conditions discussed so far, being truthful about our feelings and needs will liberate our suppressed emotions. Therefore, the tool of **reporting our anger** can be very useful. The presence and development of conditions means we have suppressed anger. It is too late to obtain the change we needed at the time we felt the anger. It is not, however, too late at least to be honest about the anger. That is how reporting the anger can help. How reporting anger differs from expressing anger is discussed after this next recap of addressing conditions of emotional dysfunction.

As the principles of emotional well-being emphasized throughout this book state, anger is a God-given emotion with a purpose. When it is expressed at the time and to the degree it is felt, anger is proportional and safe. When anger is suppressed and allowed to accumulate inside, it loses its proportionality, its integrity, and its creative properties. Unburdening ourselves from guilt requires doing *something* with the anger that is underneath the guilt. It is too late to express that anger because it already has been suppressed for so long it has developed into a condition. Therefore, the anger no longer has the capacity to *create* change. That was its potential in the beginning, but suppression has compromised that potential.

Report the Anger: Reduce the Guilt

The alternative to expressing anger is to *report* the anger. At least this liberates the anger from its participation in sustaining a dysfunctional condition. To report and thereby release (versus express) the anger, we must acknowledge the truth about:

- The lie.
- The anger.
- The fear.
- The need.

In so doing, we can say something like, "I realize I have been angry about something. Although I'm afraid to bring it up because you will find out that I lied to you, I don't want to stay angry. I also don't want this wedge to remain in my connection with you.

"So, the truth is, when you cancelled plans for that trip last year, and I told you it was all right and that I understood, that wasn't true. I was angry. I felt like you weren't accountable. You cancelled without finding out how much I was counting on the trip, and that hurt me. I tried to be flexible and understanding. Every time you asked me if it really was okay, I said yes. I *wanted* it to be okay. But it wasn't. I just didn't want to tell you the truth because I was afraid you would be angry. I've been afraid ever since that you would be angry if I told you. But now, I'd rather risk *your* anger than keep my own anger bottled up. I'd also rather tell the truth than continue to pretend."

Truth heals. It empowers. It expands our self-love, self-trust, self-respect, and self-worth. With all of those qualities engaged inside us, we have the emotional strength to survive someone else's anger. The love we feel for our self for having the courage to be truthful is much, much stronger than any anger. If we do not live in emotional integrity, we do not know how powerful love is; but if we make a commitment to emotional integrity, we soon will be able to live with new emotional power and courage within.

Being honest about our anger is the first place to regain emotional integrity. In instances of reporting our anger, that anger most likely will lack the power or integrity to change anything outwardly. However, we will definitely obtain the internal change we need. By expressing the truth, we will feel more self-love. In addition, the anger will no longer be lingering below the surface, subsidizing fear, and supporting the condition of guilt.

Anxiety and Fear

Anxiety is the condition that results from anger-based, generalized, unexpressed fear. In the beginning stages of dysfunctional emotional buildup, we suppress anger. Often we do so because of our conditioning from early-life experiences. We may have been told it is not nice to be angry. Or, in bearing the wrath of others' rage, we promised ourselves never to be like those people. We now try never to express anger. Consequently, the anger builds up inside us, and we become exactly like those people. In the process of holding our anger inside, we may not realize that accumulated anger blocks love. In fact, we may think that never showing anger, always trying to be nice, and being available to meet others' needs are the key to experiencing love. However, the opposite is true, as the anger-based patterns and conditions described in this chapter demonstrate. In addition, because of the continual buildup of anger due to suppressing our own needs, we are surely endangering our relationship with love. This accounts for the underlying fear.

The fear is that our anger is going to keep us from attracting or experiencing the quality and quantity of love we need in our lives. This kind of fear is not about our lives being in danger, which is the purpose of fear. Instead, the fear that develops from emotional dysfunction is due to our relationship with *love* being in danger. Because it is not a conscious fear, this fear that is borne of suppressed anger produces the condition of anxiety. And anxiety is the generalized condition that results when our specific fears are suppressed.

This condition can be very powerful. Nonetheless, we can reclaim our connection to love by acting on the truth of what we are doing or not doing that perpetuates not having enough love in our lives. Love is the emotion that brings us security. When we continually make choices that compromise our relationship with self-love, those outcomes cannot bring us enduring emotional security. We must replace those choices with others that are more authentic.

People pleasing and constantly believing we have to do things for others in order to maintain their friendships are good examples of choices that compromise self-love. These types of choices may be our best efforts to obtain some sense of emotional security. However, unless they are choices we love, the momentary security we experience is soon overcome by the emptiness of the truth that our efforts are designed to avoid. We are no closer to experiencing love, and the anxiety of living without adequate love persists.

Although anxiety is fear-related, it is a condition that differs significantly from the emotion of fear. Anxiety is general, non-specific, and pervasive. Without the mechanisms of emotional dysfunction engaged, however, fear is a clear, targeted emotion. In accordance with its purpose, fear lasts only for the duration of a specific threat to our lives. Then its adrenaline-pumping energies abate because there is no longer a threat to life, and our emotional equilibrium returns.

Anxiety, however, can be constant; and because it is a condition, anxiety lacks a focus. It is a general feeling of insecurity, wariness, and unease. Unsure of its cause and uncertain of its cure, we seldom think to look at our relationship with anger as the cause of our anxiety in connection with adequate love. The dysfunction producing this condition is, however, specifically related to our choices and patterns that compromise our feeling of self-love. Anger is the emotional culprit in that regard, and anger based-patterns are the source of anxiety-reducing change.

Since we have been there every moment through every enactment of every pattern that suppressed our emotions (principally, our anger), we know the truth and the consequences of the choices we have continually made. Those choices have been made principally in connection with other people. We have tried to obtain *their* love and approval because our suppressed anger has compromised our own connection with self-love. For reasons cited throughout this book, that was a flawed scheme from the onset because needing love does not attract love. Needing love attracts others who also need love. Having love within is the quality that attracts others' love to us; and when we have sufficient love within, we do not *need* love. We do, however, enjoy the expansion of love within us when that self-love attracts additional love to us.

With anxiety, the fear is that we will not be able to attract adequate love from others. The fear persists because, in some ways, it is a valid fear. To continue needing love without replenishing it within is not a model for experiencing adequate love. By changing the focus from others to self, however, we *can* begin to feel more love. The only love we can ever create is the love inside us. Therefore, we can actually reverse the anger-based anxiety by applying principles for (1) reclaiming the love within, and (2) facing the truth of the anxiety-based fears.

Reclaim the Love Within

To reclaim the love within, we must act on the self-love messages we regularly receive but ignore. Ignoring self-love messages perpetuates the anxiety of inadequate love. Anger is the emotion that has the power and inclination to ignore.

For example, the condition of anxiety is perpetuated by experiences and patterns that produce inadequate love. For these patterns to have developed the power to keep us anxiety-ridden, they have been developing a long time. In addition, they are the product of Anger Bypass™. When we expend great efforts to be nice, people-please, or meet others' needs—and those efforts do not meet our own needs (*i.e.*, we do not experience others' love as a result)—the truth is, we get angry.

The problem is, with the condition of anxiety in place, we do not feel that anger. Therefore, we do not express it—to *ourselves*. Instead, our internal Anger Bypass™ mechanism goes directly to the fear factor. "Oh, no," we think to ourselves. "That didn't work. I've got to try something else in order to attract love." And we amp up our efforts some more, and endure some more "failure" at attracting love. All the while, all the anger that gathers (because our needs are unmet) further distances us from love, taking us in the opposite direction from where our considerable efforts have intended. More importantly, our anger is completely bypassed as an agent for change.

Face the Truth

We must, therefore, reclaim our emotional integrity in order to halt this pattern. The truth is, it is not working, and we must accept and act on that truth. As familiar and established as the pattern of trying to obtain others' love is, doing for others and pleasing others in order to experience love is not the way love works. Love is within. Or, if it is *not* within us, then that is where our focus must be addressed... starting with our anger.

We must allow the truth of our anger to impact *us*. Doing so will not only halt the automatic, pervasive anxiety; it will also utilize the powerful properties of the anger to disrupt the others-directed patterns and reorganize them so we can begin to feel some relief. And some love.

The truth is, we have been angry with our self for every self-exploiting act we have committed in order to gain love from others. We can harness that unexpressed anger and direct it toward the aspect of our self that allowed those actions. In so doing, we can replace the energy in those other-directed, people-pleasing patterns and experience new ways of honoring our own needs and our own self. Only by addressing our needs and anger will we be able to meaningfully address any of the anger-based patterns that create the conditions this chapter discusses. Therefore, reducing the blocks to acting on self-care and self-love promptings is a continual objective in Transforming Anger (and anger-based patterns and conditions) Into Love™.

Rage and Emotional Detachment

> *People are like steel. When they lose their temper they lose their worth.*
>
> ~ Chuck Norris, actor

Rage is an extreme condition resulting from the long-term buildup of long-term unmet needs for love. It results from accumulated anger, combined with paralyzing fear. This product of powerful, suppressed emotions is a condition that ordinary human emotional capacities and defense mechanisms cannot possibly contain.

Rage is the extreme outcome of the extreme experience of UnLove. That term is used in this book in a specific manner. It is based on the fact that a child can be in a loving environment but not necessarily experience that love. UnLove is the result of not experiencing love. The love may have been present but the buildup of rage is an indicator of extreme unmet needs for love. That love may have been present, but it was not felt.

The combination of volatile, desperate energies constituting rage is beyond our innate capacity to hold inside. Our human emotional repertoire is not equipped to do so because our emotions are not meant to be denied. They are messages about our experience of the circumstances in our lives. If our emotional response is positive, that is a cue to continue the circumstances. If our emotional response is not positive, it lets us know it's time for change. So long as we continually monitor and modify our life circumstances so we experience love, we feel powerful and secure.

Rage results from the opposite experience and creates the opposite extreme: no love. Accordingly, rage is amotional: it is out of touch with all emotions. Rage is an automatic, out of control condition that has no emotional presence, no emotional conscience, and no capacity for remorse—at least, not at the time it is engaged. Rage is, therefore, detached from any sense of connection or belonging. It is an alienated, alienating, isolated, and isolating condition. Detached from any personal accountability or responsibility, rage is also detached from any collective conscience, accountability, or responsibility. Its only potential is to destroy. It is the one condition that can actually destroy our relationship with love, starting with self-love.

Rage is basically an enormous buildup of anger occurring over years and years. Or, for a child, it is the buildup of anger over a large portion of that child's lifespan. Continuing to suppress current anger keeps the inferno of rage fueled. Without current anger feeding it, the rage dies down. As the *Return to Love* chapter describes, when we change our patterns of suppressing anger, we simultaneously reduce the rage and the need for revenge it fosters within.

There are, thankfully, ways to reverse the cumulative patterns producing rage. The process must start with accessing the one emotion remaining that has not been ravaged by the rage. That emotion is sadness. Because sadness is humanity's emotional response to the loss or lack of love, the more love the rage destroys, the more sadness we develop. We do not experience or express that sadness if we are besieged by the condition of rage, but the sadness accumulates.

The reason we do not experience the sadness is that the rage protects us from it. That is the function of rage: it protects us from feeling the sadness that results every time the rage destroys love.

As the principles for *Transforming Anger Into Love*™ outline, accessing and releasing the sadness creates the return to love. The rage has accumulated due to the unmet need for love from others. Once we access the sadness, we are able to release the emotions built up from the lack of love from others. At the same time, we are able to commence the return to love, because the sadness shows us the way. That process is summarized in the *Withdrawal and Sadness* topic that follows.

Withdrawal and Sadness

Withdrawal is the condition that develops from the long-term suppression of sadness. In general, this non-dynamic, non-specific, emotionally unavailable condition is different from a potentially healthy emotional withdrawal. An example is emotionally withdrawing from a situation based on a specific emotional impulse. For example, we may feel angry that someone is trying to take advantage of us. We therefore pull back emotionally in an effort to become more objective, less involved, less vulnerable, and to gain a different perspective. At other times, the impulse of fear might trigger withdrawal. A new twist in an investment deal might cause us to become wary, and we withdraw in order to reconsider. The *functional* aspect of sadness might also prompt us to withdraw. We might listen to someone's story, realize it is activating a not-quite-healed place inside us, and then choose to be less empathically available in honor of our own emotional capacities and needs.

These instances are not the product of the generalized condition of withdrawal that results from the dysfunction of unexpressed sadness. These are examples of emotional integration. The first is anger related, the second is fear related, and the third is sadness related. In addition, they are all self-love-related choices. When we withdraw based on spontaneous emotional input and maintain emotional awareness as we monitor our subsequent feelings and emotional insights, this is emotional power. It differs dramatically from emotional dysfunction, as the following dysfunctional withdrawal episode depicts.

In this example, you and a new friend are meeting for lunch. You're discussing the challenges of parenting Indigo Children, and you begin to exchange stories about what each of you have tried in connection with discipline: what worked, what didn't, how your children respond differently, etc. In other words, you think it's a typical conversation between two committed, caring parents.

She tells you that she punishes her son for not getting good grades.

"My son has a genius level IQ," this mother states. "There is no reason for him not to get all A's. He just gets lazy and distracted. So we punish him when he doesn't do his best."

You, too, have a child whose intelligence is off the charts. You, too, have tried punishing him for "not doing his best." As a result, he did his worst. He did his worst so well that he almost failed that year. You sensed that he had decided to punish his parents for a punishment he felt was unfair and unwarranted. "My grades in one year of junior high are not going to be the reason I succeed or fail in life," your son said. "So after that," you confide in this lunchtime discussion, "we decided punishment was not the answer."

I Can't Stand It Any More... Again

To your dismay, although you are only casually sharing a story with this other parent, she suddenly reacts. She says she feels judged and accused. She proceeds to defend herself vigorously (against assertions you never made). After delivering her defense, she angrily puts down money for her lunch and abruptly leaves.

For purposes of this subject, she "withdraws." Is she angry? Definitely. And possibly guilt-ridden? Yes, perhaps. But she is also over-wrought with sadness inside. Dysfunctional sadness is the condition that causes us to withdraw. There may be other layers of emotional patterning at play, as this chapter discusses at length. But withdrawal is the condition of emotional dysfunction that results when we lack the emotional power and capacity to access and release accumulated sadness. Our emotional power and capacity have been forfeited in disregard of expressing our anger and needs, as the preceding examples discuss. The sadness from loss of love (especially self-love) has accumulated steadily as a result.

In the preceding example, this parent was so dysfunctional as a result of her sadness that she had no option but to completely withdraw. She was even so dysfunctional that as the sadness began to rise within her, her only emotional defense was to lash out with sufficient energy to keep the sadness at bay. Much like the function that rage serves in protecting us from sadness, irrational projections and defenses serve a similar function. They are a dysfunctionally successful effort to avoid the sadness. Therefore, they engage in an energetic pattern that is accessible and familiar: defend and run.

As an emotion with a purpose, sadness is our response to the loss or lack of love.[4] As a functional emotion, sadness is designed to be our immediate response to "self-undoing." If, for example, we suppress our anger and then express it in a manner that lacks proportionality and integrity, we are likely to say and do things we regret. Unless our suppression mechanisms have seriously compromised our emotional integrity, the instant we say or do those things, we feel sad. We regret that we have hurt someone with our words, and the sadness prompts us to heal that transgression. At that moment, if we honor the sadness, we apologize or express regret or remorse. Through our own actions, we have caused the loss of love, and our sadness engages our emotional accountability. The sadness impacts us internally because we do not love the way we just behaved. We can then reinstate self-love by being accountable.

The sadness also prompts us to impact the external situation by engaging our self-love and accountability and injecting those into the situation immediately. This combination of self-love and love for the other person enables us to repair or recover the loss of love we produced.

Without the dynamic function of sadness available to maintain our emotional equilibrium, we lose emotional security, power, and integrity. Without this return-to-love mechanism operating, we lose touch with the power to retain (or regain) connection to love. The eventual and inevitable consequence of losing that self-correcting, return-to-love mechanism is that we drift further and further away from a dynamic, emotional life. In effect, therefore, we are withdrawn from emotional responses to, and emotional participation in, daily life events.

Originally engaged due to the loss or lack of love, the sadness that accumulates becomes emotionally immobilizing and almost inexpressible. Reversing the automatic pattern of withdrawal commences with experiencing and releasing the sadness. "But I cry all the time," we sometimes report from the interior of this dysfunctional state. "If experiencing

---

[4] The lack of love originates in early life. The loss of love is due to our anger-based emotional dysfunction. In the Transforming Anger Into Love™ model, grief is our emotional response to loss of love resulting from death.

the sadness were the answer, I would have already accomplished that."

Tears of sadness and tears of depression are significantly different, however. Sadness is our response to the loss of love, and its purpose is to expand our potential for love so that when the sadness is released, we are left with a greater capacity to experience love. If we behave in a manner that creates loss of love and our sadness lets us know that, then, as it occupies our emotional repertoire, feeling the sadness is a prompting that urges us to return to love. After the sadness is released, our emotional cavity has been expanded by its presence, and we are left with a greater capacity to experience love.

The functional connection between sadness and love is immediate and direct. The accumulation of sadness is like a large database. It holds in it a memory of everything that has resulted in the loss of love—everything we have said or done, or not said or not done, that has produced the loss of love. The sadness also holds the information for how to reverse the patterns that have produced that loss. Therefore, if we cry from the sadness, we are in touch with the loss of love. The sadness reveals to us the patterns that have produced loss of love, and the insights for how to change those patterns in order to reclaim our connection with love—starting with self-love. The love-related insights available when we access the sadness provide the specific steps to reverse our dysfunctional patterns and conditions.

If we cry from the depression, we do not see the patterns and answers related to loss of love. We often do not even know why we are crying when we are depressed. Tears of depression are based on anger because our needs for love are not met. We cannot see the pathway to love so long as we are covering it with unexpressed, denied anger. With depression, our anger-based patterns have accumulated to the degree that they compromise our relationship with love. But because we continue to suppress anger, our needs are not met, and our relationship with love is not dynamically expanding. In this stage of depressed emotional dysfunction, although we know the truth of what we are doing to compromise love, our anger locks us into the patterns that regularly and regrettably compromise our experience of love.

As other writing in this book suggests, accessing the emotional courage to experience and release the sadness commences the return to love. The chapters *Transforming Anger Into Love*™ and *Return to Love* offer guidelines for reversing the various conditions that are described in this chapter. Reversing the condition of withdrawal begins with honoring the message about love that the sadness offers. The sadness has accumulated from the loss of love from others. It has been perpetuated from the conditions discussed. The withdrawal is the result of feeling we lack the capacity to experience the love we need. So long as we continue needing love from others, that pattern is validated. But if we follow the return-to-love message from the sadness, the sadness will cease accumulating. Then we can experience the dynamic renewal of love, starting with self-love.

For too long, we have avoided the sadness, thinking that its accumulation was too painful to face. However, the pain of facing the sadness is not nearly so great as the pain of continuing to live without experiencing adequate love. Until the reversal of the love-endangering patterns begins, we cannot possibly know the outcomes that are possible when we actually face the sadness. While we were in the process of perpetuating rather than reversing the patterns and conditions of emotional dysfunction, the outcomes were indeed limited. When we do access the storehouse of sadness accumulated due to the loss of love, we see through the patterns we have perpetuated—the patterns that have continually compromised our relationship with love.

Those insights enable us to change the patterns that block our connection with love and they show us the steps to Return to Love.

Chapter Seven

Return To Love

If you try to look, but you don't touch,
Then you might touch, but you'll never feel,
And if you don't feel, you'll never cry,
And if you don't cry, you'll never heal.

If You Try To Look[6]
By Harry Chapin

Although the automatic patterns of emotional suppression are powerful, they can be reversed. This is undoubtedly the most hopeful message of the principles for Transforming Anger Into Love™. The patterns have accumulated because of unexpressed anger and our unmet need for love from others. When we transform these patterns we no longer perpetuate the unmet need for love from others. We meet the long-term unmet need for self-love.

The steps to transform these patterns begin with accessing the sadness. It is the emotion we have accumulated in response to loss of love, and it is the emotion we must access in order to return to love.

Sadness: The Suppressed and the Functional

As the chapter on *Conditions of Emotional Dysfunction* describes, each of the four principal emotions develops into a non-dynamic condition if it is consistently suppressed. With sadness, the resulting condition is withdrawal.[1] Prior to that development, the patterns of suppression are evident in subtle ways. For example, if we have suppressed sadness inside, we release it by crying... too often.

- We cry too often at movies.
- We cry too often in everyday conversations.
- We frequently overreact when we read a news story about a child or a family or an animal.
- We can't pick out a sympathy card without emotionally falling apart.

These are indicators of suppressed sadness because the responses are out of proportion and out of control. It is understandable that we sometimes cry at movies. It is healthy to be empathic and sensitive, and to care about the plight of those who are vulnerable. If our sadness is out of control, however, an event may trigger our sadness, but it is not the source of our sadness. If too many events trigger too much sadness, we are responding from suppressed sadness, not current, functional sadness.

Since sadness is our response to the loss of love (or in childhood, it is

---

[1] If our children develop a tendency to withdraw emotionally and that reaction persists, that is an indication of suppressed sadness. If they burst into tears at almost everything, and that reaction persists, that is an indication of suppressed sadness. If their anger builds up to the degree it is frequently out of control, that buildup is an indication of rage. Rage destroys love, including self-love. Therefore, while the rage is a mechanism to avoid experiencing the sadness, it is also a factor in accumulating the sadness. The previous chapters describe the Rage/Sadness Axis™ in greater detail.

the response to inadequate love, or lack of love), if our sadness is functional, it is temporary and soon replaced with love. For example, we can be in a loving relationship, but over time, our needs may change. Although there may be considerable love in the relationship, we know we must end it because it no longer meets our needs. As the relationship is ending, and even for a period of time afterwards, we will undoubtedly feel sad.

But the legacy of that relationship is love. We now have more love inside us than we did before, and that is the enduring value of the relationship. After the sadness has been released, every time we think of that person we will experience the love activated within us, not the loss of that person's presence in our life. The sadness is a healthy, appropriate response to the loss. However, like anger and fear, sadness is not designed to be an enduring emotion. It is our emotional *response* to loss of love. It is not the automatic outcome of loss of love. Even if we lose connection with the person, we never lose the love. For that reason, sadness is a temporary emotional response that is designed to be expressed and released so it can be replaced by the presence of love.

Love is the enduring emotion. It is always within us in the form of self-love. In addition, *any* love we have *ever* experienced is always with us. Every person who has loved us, and every person we have loved, all have increased our experience of love. That is the enduring property of love.

Even though it is connected to loss of love, the gift of sadness is that it actually expands our capacity to experience love. The presence of the sadness holds a space for the reclaimed love to fill. That occurs when we follow the guidance of the sadness and we do reconnect with love.

When we *experience* the sadness, its message guides us back to love. When we *suppress* sadness, however, the accumulation insulates us from love. The greater the amount of suppressed sadness, the greater the insulation and distance from love. For these reasons, it is important to identify and face our suppressed sadness. Despite all our efforts to diminish our anger and increase our relationship with love, if our anger has created loss of love, and we have not released the sadness, the sadness remains an obstacle on the pathway for returning to love.

It is important to understand that need to suppress, however, because it was a vital survival mechanism at some point… in early life. As children, our sadness is often the emotional response to inadequate love. We suppress the sadness because our emotional capacity as little children is incapable of accommodating it. We feel the overwhelming sadness of being in an emotionally inadequate environment. We also conclude that living with that sadness for many more years will be unsurvivable. So we shut off our access to the sadness. It continues to accumulate in that environment; and the suppression mechanism continues to grow more and more powerful. But at least we do not have to face the "truth" we fear: that we are not loved (adequately) because we are not lovable.

Sadness and the Truth

The reason so many of us are unwilling to face our sadness is that we expect to experience that "truth" from early life extended into adulthood as: "There is not enough love to meet my needs." If we have a storehouse of sadness, we have that belief and fear. So long as we can suppress the sadness, we are able to avoid that belief and fear being confirmed. We are unable to keep them out of our consciousness entirely, however, because they are only suppressed. Because of that, they seep into our thoughts from time to time when we think:

- I didn't have enough love.
- I don't have enough love.
- I won't have enough love.
- There isn't enough love.
- I can't count on love being there.
- I'm never going to get what I need.
- It's my fault.
- I'm not lovable.

These are all indicators of suppressed sadness based on untruthful belief and untruthful fear. When we access the sadness we have been avoiding for so long, however, we see how these beliefs and fears were formed. In addition, the sadness reveals *the truth* about love, about being lovable, and about the environment that was so incapable of providing the love we needed.

We see the truth of the *others'* emotional inadequacy in early life. Unlike what we had concluded, we see that we are not unlovable. We even see the patterns that have caused us to feel unlovable, and the patterns that have caused us to continue perpetuating the experience of inadequate love. We see that those patterns are not the truth of who we are. We also see how changing those patterns can attract the love we need and enable us to experience the love we have needed most: self-love.

Release the Sadness

Accessing the sadness is a profound and profoundly healing experience. All the love we have lost touch with is stored in that body of suppressed sadness. When we connect with it, for that one powerful healing moment, it doesn't matter that had we experienced the sadness before, all of this love would have been with us ever since. When we commence the Return to Love, we don't feel the sadness. We only feel the love that we had lost touch with and now are able to experience, all at once. To experience this love and truth brings us to the end of a long, long journey.

Until that moment occurs, we are still in the wake of our emotional dysfunction. We have been there for so long, and we have avoided the sadness for such good reasons, it may be difficult to trust that facing what we've avoided is the answer to what we need.

After following the guidelines in this book and becoming aware of the patterns that emotional suppression creates, it will be easier. These guidelines offer new awareness about the origin of sadness, its purpose, and its presence. They also offer assurance that experiencing the sadness is a healing experience that enables us to reconnect with love.

We often know the sadness is underneath, but we do not know how to release it. The preceding chapters in this book have begun to activate that release. Now our challenge is to avoid suppressing the sadness as it begins to emerge. Even if we are in the grocery store and the sadness wells up, it is ready to be released, and we must honor that. Something we are doing, or thinking about, or feeling, is allowing the sadness to emerge. If our first reaction is to hide it because of what others might think, that is a familiar, automatic suppression mechanism that we must override. We must trust the sadness and value it more than the opinion of strangers we will never see again. The sadness is being released so that we can reclaim our relationship with love. Nothing is more important.

As we do begin to release the sadness, we will recall incidents in our past that produced the loss or lack of love. The sadness is showing us those incidents so that we can change similar patterns that are operating in our lives now. To facilitate those changes, we will be able to use the powerful destroyer companion of anger: rage.

Utilize the Rage

Once that sadness is released, the emotional reversal is underway. As the diagram at the beginning of this chapter details, the next step in the Return to Love is to address the rage. The preceding chapters in this book discuss how and why the accumulation of suppressed sadness is connected to rage. The rage may be internalized, it may be externalized, or it is likely to be both. Any form of self-destructive, uncontrolled, uncontrollable behavior is the result of anger accumulated along the Anger/Rage Axis™. Once the sadness is released, and the Return to Love begins, the rage diminishes, based on three important principles:

- The destructive properties of rage can be dismantled by directing its formerly destructive energies toward the aspects of ourselves we do not love;
- Because rage is an accumulation of the anger from UnLove in the past, once we connect with the love available by accessing the sadness, the chamber accommodating the rage will dissolve; and
- Because the rage has been fueled by automatic patterns of suppressing anger, once we cease suppressing our anger, the rage will cease.

These Rage Reversal™ principles are essential to the Return to Love. They utilize the accumulated reservoir of destructive emotional energy in a positive manner. If that emotional energy is not utilized or transformed, it will retain its properties as Engagable Rage™. Then, although certain positive changes may occur for a limited period of time, the sabotaging energies of the rage will re-emerge. These potentially destructive energies can now be appropriated and directed in a positive manner because they are stewarded from the presence of self-love. The conditions occasioning and accumulating them are no longer present. As the sadness is released, the love it has stored also releases. With that, the rage can cease. The connection to love has occurred.

To utilize these potent energies, we can direct them toward the aspects of ourselves that we want to replace: people-pleasing, using money to impress others, and obsessing about our body and appearance, for example. We can now become angry with those aspects because we are not embedded in the suppressive patterns that perpetuated them. We may have wanted to make these changes in the past. We may have even felt anger or self-contempt for the unproductive patterns and outcomes we perpetuated. But we did not have the capacity to make changes based on self-love. We also did not know how to transform the rage, so it remained.

After we have engaged the rage in our Return to Love, we can confront the next layer of suppressed emotions that threatened our relationship with love: fear.

Risk the Fear

Mark Twain once said, "I'm an old man and I've had a lot of problems, most of which never occurred." In his inimitable way, Twain was portraying the way many of us relate to fear. We worry about outcomes that never occur. This is certainly true in connection with suppressed anger. We often fear that expressing our anger will compromise our relationship with love. When the Return to Love model is engaged, suppressed anger has already so severely compromised our relationship with love that it is imperative we stop suppressing the anger. Fearing the consequences of continuing to suppress our anger must be greater than the fear of expressing it.

Now that we have the experience of self-love, we can make that change because we know the toll that suppression takes on our emotional integrity and well-being. In addition, having now experienced the joy and security of self-love, we know to fear any pattern that jeopardizes that love. More important, we now have the capacity to utilize fear as a signal that our unproductive patterns are threatening our connection to self-love.

Until we have the experience of connecting with all the love the sadness has stored, our fear may still be so compromised it does not reliably tell us when we have something to fear and when we do not. When our fear has been suppressed and denied, it can become a generalized, unfocused condition occasioned by the fear of inadequate love. Until we connect with the love that the sadness reveals, that anger-related fear factor renders our responses unreliable, and unproductive.

Those same fear-based patterns may be activated as they are targeted for transformation in the Return to Love. This time, they will be challenged to distinguish the truth between whether our relationship with love is in danger, or whether these unproductive patterns are in danger. If the Return to Love model is working, it will target those patterns by challenging their presence and purpose.

Our strongest weapon against fear at any time is to ask, "What is the truth?" If our fear is functional and reliable, it will reveal exactly what we are to fear, why, and what steps to take to avoid compromising our relationship with love. As we follow the guidance for the Return to Love and the fear-based patterns engage, we can ask our self:

- What is the truth?
- Are the changes I am making adding to my emotional power and confidence?
- Are they revealing the past patterns and replacing them with authenticity and self-love? Do I feel better about myself as I make these changes?
- Or do I want to go back to the patterns?
- Which do I fear the most?

Real fear responds to the truth. It tells us what to fear and why. Defense mechanisms were engaged based on fear of the truth. Their function was to protect us from the fear of being unlovable. When we connect with love, those defenses dissolve. Therefore, as we apply these principles and our fear tries to paralyze us from taking the actions to Return to Love, that is surely an old pattern deserving of our self-loving application of "rage."

Transform the Anger

As we accessed the sadness, we saw that the pattern of continually suppressing anger was continually fueling the rage. We had regularly feared that our rage would continue to destroy our potential for attracting love. Now, thankfully, we see that we can eliminate the pattern sustaining the rage. As we now employ the Return to Love model to reverse the powerful patterns of suppression, we follow the diagram at the beginning of this chapter. We start with the sadness; then we address the rage; then the fear; then the anger; and then we are able to sustain our relationship with love. We learn to experience the sadness to reconnect us with love. We learn to employ the rage with self-love, and dismantle patterns and aspects of ourselves that we were unable to trust and love. We learn to utilize the fear as a signal that our connection to self-love is being threatened by the presence of old, unproductive patterns. Next we learn to utilize the anger to create the changes we need in order to experience and sustain the connection with self-love.

All of these patterns were created in connection with needing love from others. As each emotion is utilized to reverse the suppressive patterns, that emotion is integrated into dynamic, spontaneous, emotional power... and we love that experience. We love being back in touch with our emotions. We love the experience of the automatic patterns being replaced with new emotional options. We begin to love the self that has summoned the courage to face the truth.

With these layers of accumulated emotional energy transformed, we are now reconnecting with love, and we can be back in touch with spontaneous, proportional, trustworthy anger. We can now trust our anger to signify when our needs are not met. Ideally, when that occurs, we will be able to access the self-love within to respond with compassion or patience. Otherwise, we can now trust expressing our anger. It can be an important tool for challenging the untapped potential in a situation so that it meets our needs. Or, the anger can be a signal that we may need to change situations. Either way, by trusting our anger, we halt the destructive pattern of accumulating it. We reinstate the power of anger to create what we need. And, as a result, we are able to experience more love.

Experience the Love

We love the feeling we have inside as we apply these new principles. We love the person we become as we reverse these unproductive patterns. We love the choices we make and we love the courage that emerges as we say the truth of what we feel and what we need. In the process, we become someone others can love and trust. As we gather more and more love inside, we attract others who have love inside. We not only have self-love inside to cherish and protect. We also have reliable emotional options to let us know when we are doing or saying something that puts our self-love at risk.

With self-love inside, we have returned to love. We are the love we need.

Notes

Chapter Eight

The Hidden Power of Love™

When anger is expressed at the time it is felt, its purpose is to challenge love. When it is suppressed and allowed to accumulate, its presence takes a toll on love. The following contrasts the properties of love to the properties of suppressed anger. Reflect on how each manifests in your own life, and how to replace the effects of suppressed anger with the power and presence of love.

Love is the facilitating emotion.
Anger is the obstructing emotion.
Love produces the creativity to get things done.
Anger delays and wastes time and resources.

Love is sensitive and attentive.
Anger neglects and disregards.
Love tells the truth.
Anger avoids, denies, manipulates, and lies.

Love admits when it does not know.
Anger wants to be right.
Love admits its mistakes.
Anger is afraid to be wrong.

Love is available to listen.
Anger controls by talking.
Love has time.
Anger wants its way immediately.

Love thinks of reasons why something will work.
Anger thinks of reasons why something will fail.
Love is accountable.
Anger makes excuses.

Love provides.
Anger consumes.
Love gives.
Anger takes.

Love accepts.
Anger finds fault.
Love teaches.
Anger punishes.

Love considers.
Anger blames.
Love allows.
Anger demands.

Love accommodates.
Anger resists.
Love is generous.
Anger is needy.

Love trusts.
Anger doubts.
Love stays.
Anger leaves.

Love heals.
Anger abuses.
Love creates.
Anger destroys.

Notes

Chapter Nine

Riddled with Ritalin:
When Emotional Integrity and Emotional Maturity Are at Risk

Kid Control

"We are raising a generation of children, many of whom... understand that they have been given pills instead of love, understanding, or attention.

Most, of course, will not realize what they are missing from other people. They will assume that adults are supposed to give pills to children instead of giving them psychological and spiritual support. The children will end up blaming themselves for wanting more love and attention than they have been given."

Talking Back to Ritalin
By Peter R. Breggin, M.D.

It is impossible to discuss the emotional life of Indigo Children and not address the controversy that the drug Ritalin has stirred. In addition, I suggest that the use and effects of Ritalin deserve re-examination because the drug breaches the issues of emotional integrity.

Repeated throughout the literature and experience of Indigo Children is that they require and aspire to high standards of integrity. Ritalin robs them of that in significant ways. Notwithstanding the relief this drug has brought to many—children, parents, and teachers especially—the quality of that relief, and the short- as well as long-term consequences accompanying it, are seriously in question. Ritalin isn't the only drug widely used to control children's behavior, but it is the focus of this writing because at least, through the efforts of Dr. Peter Breggin, it has been brought to the forefront for reconsideration.

Thanks to the controversial and groundbreaking books by Dr. Breggin, two of which are quoted in this chapter, the medical community, researchers, educators, and mental health professionals are examining the use and effects of Ritalin and other kid-controlling drugs. For those who are unfamiliar with the heated Ritalin-related discussions occurring in the literature and media, the information in this chapter will help. I strongly suggest that you also become familiar with these two books by Dr. Breggin, *Talking Back to Ritalin* and *the Ritalin Fact Book*. Dr. Breggin's leadership is bold, his writing is riveting, and his soul is speaking in behalf of the health and well-being of all children and families.

The Controversy Grows

"Inspired in part by the publication of the first edition of *Talking Back to Ritalin* in 1998, the controversy surrounding the medicating of America's children has grown at a rapid rate.

Many more people now understand that something is wrong when society finds it expedient to give psychoactive chemicals to millions of children. They suspect that the diagnosis of Attention Deficit Hyperactive Disorder (ADHD) may be little more than an excuse for giving drugs to control children instead of meeting their genuine needs. They believe that our children require improved family, school, and community life rather than psychiatric diagnoses and psychoactive drugs.

In the mid-1950s, Ritalin (methylphenidate) and Dexedrine (dextroamphetamine) became the first two stimulants approved for the control of behavior in children. Later Desoxyn and Gradumet (both forms of methamphetamine) were approved. Amid a great deal of marketing promotion, Adderall has recently been added to the market. Despite the hype about its newness, Adderall is a mixture of four closely related forms of old-fashioned amphetamines and differs little from Dexedrine. Most recently, Metadate and Concerta have been approved. They are longer-acting preparations of Ritalin (methylphenidate).

All of these drugs are amphetamine-like (Ritalin, Metadate, and Concerta) or they are outright amphetamines (Adderall, Dexedrine, Desoxyn, Gradumet). For most purposes, they can be considered as one class of drug with a similar adverse reaction profile, including a high potential for addiction and abuse.

For example, each of them has been placed in Schedule II of the Drug Enforcement Administration (DEA). Schedule II—which also includes cocaine, opium, morphine, and the most dangerous barbiturates—is intended for drugs with the most extreme abuse and addiction potential. On this basis alone, stimulant drugs should never be considered benign.

Another stimulant, Cylert (pemoline), is not as addictive or prone to abuse, but has unique dangers, including fatal liver toxicity."

Excerpted from
Talking Back to Ritalin

According to author Jan Tober: "If your child:
- Has high degree of sensitivity.
- Has excessive amounts of energy.
- Bores easily.
- Appears to have a short attention span.
- Resists authority that is not democratically oriented.
- Cannot sit still unless absorbed in something of his or her own interest.
- Is very compassionate.
- Has many fears, such as death or the loss of loved ones.

"These are all signs of a potentially gifted Indigo Child."[3]

Consider, then, the implications of these two authorities' statements. The characteristics Dr. Breggin exposes as being considered drug-worthy, Tober acknowledges as being potentially gifted! Tober also says that, according to the National Foundation for Gifted and Creative Children, "Many gifted children are thought to be learning disabled. They are being falsely labeled with Attention Deficit Disorder or Attention Deficit Hyperactive Disorder, when in fact, these children are potentially gifted."[3]

Tober's co-author, Lee Carroll adds:

"Schools are designed to teach left-brained learning. That's sequential learning. I believe most gifted children, like ADD children, are right-brained, visual learners, and these kids are not going to be able to cope in this kind of learning environment. That's why so many gifted children are labeled 'problem children' and wind up being given drugs like Ritalin to make them more 'compatible' with what is considered the norm...

"They should be **studied**, not drugged."[3]

What's a Teacher To Do?

Indigo Children *are* highly gifted. They are highly sensitive. They are highly intelligent, including emotionally. Theirs are qualities to value, preserve, and incorporate in every aspect of life we possibly can. It is sometimes too simple and too early, I suggest, to turn these precious Beings over to drugs. Instead, we elders have an opportunity to turn inward and find ways to help these children emotionally, not chemically.

According to Dr. Breggin, "Among the nation's 50 million school-age children, 4-6 million are probably being exposed at any given time to stimulant drugs... Studies have shown that at least 15-20 percent of fourth and fifth-grade *boys* in public schools are receiving these [stimulant] drugs."[4]

Why? Why are so many of our children on drugs? There are undoubtedly many reasons. Parents turn to drugs because other strategies have not worked. Physicians prescribe drugs because the kids and parents need help and drugs are one option. Teachers, too, suggest drugs. They often do so as an alternative to requiring a child to change schools. Teachers feel they cannot meet their commitment to the rest of the classroom if they allow one child to disrupt the attention and learning span of the others.

In addition, teachers are not given the training and competency required to manage the emotional and behavioral conditions that kids bring to the classrooms these days. Teachers are often underpaid, usually overworked, and sorely lacking the resources they need in order to do the job they want to do. Whether it is teachers' responsibility to be an emotional and behavioral influence in kids' lives these days is a moot question. The kids show up. They're in the classrooms. They come with a lot of needs and challenges. What's a teacher to do?

Many school children (including some Indigo Children I have worked with, and know of) have been neglected and abused at home. Many school children lack an adequate role model at home or anywhere else in their lives. Their needs are so unmet that this condition comes out in the classroom. These children, much like Indigo Children, often lack the patience and interest to sit still. Often, their need is not for intellectual stimulation. They frequently need the basics: attention, nurturing, support, and the experience of being something other than a bother and a burden. The children with such needs often, and often unwittingly, project these conditions onto the teacher.

Bring into this mix a robust, self-confident, "I know all this stuff anyway" Indigo Child and it's a potion for combustion. Indigo Children can be awesomely intelligent. Their innate wisdom and range of interests can be disarming. Put them in a "learning environment" and they often want to talk about what they already know, and *what* they want to learn, and *how* they want to learn. Their minds are so filled with so many ideas and insights, they often want to share. They want to discuss. They want to ask questions, and learn what others have to say on subjects not taught in the classroom.

I often recommend to parents that they explain to their children about needs, and which environments can meet which needs, and explain the "contract" that schools have with children. Specifically, this means that there are certain needs the school and teachers can meet, and certain needs they cannot meet. If children cannot get their socialization needs met in the classroom, that does put more responsibility on the parents. So I suggest to parents that they challenge their children to figure out which needs can be met in the classroom, which ones cannot, and then support the children in figuring out a way to be in the classroom according to "the contract."

This is not a simple task to accomplish because many Indigo Children are "wired" for stimulation. With some coaching, however, these children often are able to adapt remarkably once the focus is shifted from discipline and punishment and "can't," to strategy, outwitting and, as one parent described his son's new adjustment, "flying below the radar screen."

There are also alternatives and options that will help teachers with these challenges.

1. **Share Information.** Teachers can meet together (or email one another) and share information and strategies for working with Indigo Children in the classroom. "When can we fit *that* in?" a group of teachers asked once when I was brainstorming with them. Although I do realize the time constraints every teacher faces, I do maintain that teachers are often their own best resources. They spontaneously try something with a child, it works, and they suggest it to other teachers. This happens all the time. With Indigo Children, and others who are diagnosed ADD/ADHD, teachers can agree to seek out information, and share strategies that work, then come together for 20 minutes every two weeks to share that information.

   With the group of teachers I mentioned earlier, I found out that the guidance counselor did not even know the term "Indigo Child," nor did that counselor know that these teachers felt they had a unique challenge in their classrooms. The teachers promptly engaged the counselor to look for local resources, so it is important for teachers to let counselors and others know they could use some help.

2. **Team Up with Parents.** Teachers can ask parents to help locate books, articles, lectures, workshops, and Internet-available information. Many parents of Indigo Children are quite energetic in seeking out information and resources. These parents also share with one another. If a group of teachers shows an interest in learning more about managing these special children in the classroom, it's likely the parents will be grateful, and helpful.

3. **Consult Local Colleges, Universities, and Schools.** If there is a college or university in your area, tap the professors. Call the medical school and see if there are teaching physicians who lecture about or do research on gifted children. Also contact schools for the gifted and talented, and private schools. (For information, see the *Resources* list at the end of this book.) In a metropolitan area, other public schools may have teachers and counselors who

can help. Check also with practitioners and therapists. They also may know of resources, including ones in your area.

4. **Adult Teachers of Indigo Children.** My colleague, Jeanne Kayser, once suggested, half in jest, that we form a self-help group for Adult Parents of Indigo Children. We have not done that yet, but I strongly suggest trying it. I get calls every week from parents who want someone else to talk with. They also want to find other Indigo Children for their own children to interact with. I receive calls from school guidance counselors, too. Often, they are seeking anger management help for a student. But after talking with the counselor, I frequently realize they are describing an Indigo Child. It could therefore be extremely beneficial for adults to create a self-help group. The group could include teachers, as well. They could interactively support one another and offer suggestions from their own what-worked, what-didn't repertoire. They could also locate, share, and even create resources. Enlisting the children to create resources is also a good idea.

From the files of what-doesn't-work with Indigo Children, the following are comments from one who knows, one who cares, and one who is on the front lines of these situations every day.

From Robert P. Ocker, teacher:

"Punishment will not work with these kids. It establishes fear, requires judgment, creates intentions of anger, and invites more conflict. These children will withdraw, rebel, and sink inward with hate. This is dangerous for their souls and for the lives of others. Avoid punishment!

Discipline guides children by providing logical and realistic consequences. It shows what they have done wrong, gives them ownership of the problem, offers them ways to solve the problem they created, and leaves their dignity intact.

Experiencing logical and realistic consequences teaches the Indigo Child that they have positive control over their lives and that they can make decisions and solve their own problems. The children want this guidance. It empowers their royal and wise nature and gives them the power to be responsible, resourceful, and caring individuals. It allows them to be Who They Are!

These children demand dignity and worth. They read your intent more than your words. They are wise in their souls, young in their hearts."[1]

Ocker says don't punish them. Breggin says don't drug them. Carroll says study them...

What's a Parent To Do?

Indigo Children's needs can be intense. Their behavior can be unmanageable. Their emotions can be overpowering, for them and for us. Often, the unmanageable aspects are connected to anger, and one option is to suppress their behavior with drugs. But that option suppresses their emotional essence and affect, as well. We must, therefore, find another way. Dr. Breggin states that love is not enough if loving parents' lack of moral authority allows their children to run rampant. "The expression of love gradually becomes lost amid the chaos created by the now out-of-control children."[4]

"When anger is the problem, the needs are primarily emotional, and the challenge may be primarily behavioral, but the answer is not, primarily pharmaceutical...

"We, as elders in these children's lives, have greater untapped potential for love than we are experiencing and expressing. That is one of the essential messages about the presence of Indigo Children in our lives. They are here for a purpose. A large purpose. In addition to the inventions they will leave behind and the future they will help create, they have an unmistakable capacity for love: for experiencing it, expressing it, recognizing it, and for inspiring and assisting us in facing the aspects of our lives that restrict our own relationship with love... which includes examining our own relationship with anger."

~ Dianne Lancaster
September 28, 2002 Workshop
Anger and the Indigo Child

Creating more love is the purpose of Transforming Anger Into Love™. It is a body of principles and information that addresses anger-based patterns because anger is the principal emotion that restricts our relationship with love. If our own anger is formatted in automatic patterns, our own emotional potential is restricted. We create an Anger Grid™ in interacting with our children. When we reach our limit in those interactions, we do not have any other emotional capacities or options. We may, then, consider turning to a chemical solution for our children's emotional and physical outbursts.

However, if we can unlock those patterns within ourselves, and unleash the emotional potential we have foreclosed, we will have greater capacity for meeting our children's needs rather than artificially suppressing them.

We compromise our own emotional power when we manipulate our own anger. We manipulate our anger when it wells up inside us and we don't acknowledge it, or express it, or don't transform it with the love from inside us.[1]

The alternative to expressing or manipulating our anger is to reroute it. Rerouting anger without expressing it is perfect, in fact, if we reroute the anger into our capacity for love. For example, let's say we are relaxed after dinner and finally catching up on a stack of reading when our 12-year old announces she needs a certain kind of poster board for a school project. "And it's due tomorrow," she adds, "so we have to get to the mall before it closes."

Most of us are unable to say unconditionally at a time like that, "How fun! Let's go right now!" Occasionally, however, we can resist our first impulse, which is something like:

- "Why didn't you tell me this earlier?"
- "How long have you known about this?"
- "Why can't you use some of the other kinds of paper we've bought you for school?"

---

[1] Since we sometimes think we have "transformed" our anger by letting the moment go by without blasting someone, it is important to make the following distinction: When anger is transformed, love returns immediately. The anger is completely neutralized by the love, and we never again think about the incident. Otherwise, we deny the anger, and we think about the incident over and over again. That is suppression, not transformation. Transformation completely reconfigures the energy of anger. Suppression only exiles it into an internal reservoir where it accumulates, gathers momentum, and eventually emerges in an unproportional, unproductive manner.

- "Can't you borrow that kind of paper from John, who lives down the street?"
- "Can't you ask your mother to take you?"
- "Can't you tell the teacher… something… ?"

Our internal-if-not-spoken response is usually:
- "Why does it always go this way?"
- "When will she ever learn?"
- "How in the world can she possibly think she's going to get through life this way?"
- "When *I* was her age, *I* would have… "

When we reroute the anger, and access the love inside, that love speaks to us and says: "She's 12, for heaven's sake! She's a great kid. She works hard in school. She's responsible. I can read weeks-old magazines later."

Rerouting anger doesn't keep it from coming up. But if we practice this option, it does give us an opportunity to consciously access an emotional alternative. When we are able to successfully reroute the anger so that it activates the love inside, we walk to the car without adding the silent dramatics we've used before to let her know, "This is very, very inconvenient." Instead, we are able to take advantage of the time alone and ask, sincerely, "How *are* you doing in school? What are you doing in this new project?"

These are the moments we cherish. And mostly, we cherish them within. Surely nothing is more joyful or powerful than to have the capacity for unconditional love.

I'm Not Angry

There are times when we may not have the capacity for unconditional love. Our own lives and needs are too consuming, and our own stresses and frustrations are too great. Those are the "say things we don't mean" moments. We later find ourselves thinking, "I wish I had been more available. I wish I hadn't been quite so impatient. I wish I could take back the words and tone of voice that my child really didn't deserve. To this day, I really feel bad about those times."

We have those regrets periodically, yet, when they come up, we still don't say we're sorry. Anger is the reason. It isn't just the flame-thrower moments that cause damage. It isn't just the times we didn't apologize that cause our anger to take a toll—although that would have helped. Anger is much more pernicious than that… if it is manipulated, that is. If anger is expressed at the moment it is felt, it is released and we never think of that moment again. Releasing anger in that manner gives integrity to the common, automatic response: "Oh, it's okay. It didn't matter. I don't mind. It worked out just fine." It's not okay if you keep thinking about it. And if you think about it again and again, it's *really* not okay. You're still angry.

That is why the issue of emotional integrity is so important. If we, the elders, do not honor our own emotional integrity, we are not bothered as much by impugning our children's. If we don't love and honor and trust our own feelings, we are less likely to value and protect theirs.

For the Children's Sake

"But these kids are unmanageable. There are diagnoses to prove it," say the parents of children whose volatility keeps the entire family's world in chaos. For those parents, there are immediate and compelling reasons to suppress their children's uncontrolled moods and behaviors. I, however, suggest that because there are long-term consequences of emotional development we are not factoring, we are often gravely mismanaging this issue by drugging the children. The opportunity is ours, therefore, to raise our emotional standards, not to artificially control and lower theirs. As Dr. Breggin, states, "Stimulants do not correct 'biochemical imbalances'—they cause them."[4]

Besides, whether the children's emotional development is suppressed with drugs or with emotional dysfunction, the consequences extend even beyond those described in the preceding paragraphs. As many practitioners and healing methods regularly confirm, suppressed emotional energy exiled into the body creates significant physical messages, symptoms, and dis-ease. Acupuncture and Oriental Medicine have treated the energy-storage systems in the body for centuries. Some of the outstanding contemporary authors also contributing to our understanding of the body/emotion connection include Louise Hay, Michio Kushi, Letha Hadady, Stanley Keleman, Naboru Muramoto, and Linda Rector Page.

Even more consequences of emotional suppression are detailed in this book's chapter on *Emotions, Energy and the Body: A Guide to Symbology, Meaning and Understanding* and in *Conditions of Emotional Dysfunction*. That chapter adds significantly to the understanding of patterns that form, and grids that result, from the continual denial and suppression of anger. From the anger angle, emotional dysfunction has a dramatic effect on the body's energy flow and chemical balance. Therefore, returning to *emotional* equilibrium and well-being complements the body's ability to regain its own physical balance and harmony. Long-term, cumulative emotional dysfunction, on the other hand, takes a commensurate toll on the body's natural capacity to regain that balance.

The experts and literature differ on exactly what positive contribution (if any) Ritalin makes on the body's chemistry and energy connectivity. It is, however, possible that positively impacting the patterns that produce *emotional* outbursts will likewise positively impact the physical and energetic outbursts. This has, in fact, been my experience in working with many, many Indigo Children and families, and the results often have been profound.

I remember, for example, the domestic violence call I received from a hospital emergency room. The hospital staff had called in the police because a sister had hit her brother so hard that the parents had taken him in for immediate treatment. The daughter was on the verge of being arrested when the mother asked that the hospital call me first. At that time, the mother and I had only talked about my working with the family. But since the mother had at least made an attempt at getting help previously, the police were willing to consider anger management in lieu of automatic arrest.

The young woman was often violent at home, I discovered. Her brother was the one whom she physically assaulted most often. She kept the entire family on constant alert, however. She blew up several times a day. They had tried several medications, including anti-depressants, but they suspected she had not taken them as prescribed, because none had seemed to make any difference at all.

The daughter was almost debilitated by severe, ongoing headaches. Her teeth were ground down so severely from stress (anger) that the dentist was not even sure he could do anything but replace them. Because she ground her teeth all night long, the young woman never got a good night's rest. "I lie there all night and dread the next day," she said when I asked once, "What goes through your mind when you lie awake for hours, night after night?"

One point from losing her driver's license because of so many speeding tickets, and drifting back and forth from one abusive relationship to another, this young woman was also on the verge of losing her after-school job. Her temper was so bad at work, other family members confided, that once she upended her desk and stormed out. She had not been fired yet because her employer was a friend of the family. Everyone involved in the situation was on edge, however, not sure they were making the right choices, and definitely afraid of making a wrong one.

After a few weeks of learning how to reverse the patterns of rage, she was a changed human being. After a few months, we all agreed, she had turned her emotional dysfunctions around. When we had begun to work together, I had confirmed that she simply needed to be taught another way to understand and manage her uncontrollable emotions. She was exceptionally bright, and accustomed to "understanding everything." What bothered her the most, she said, was that she couldn't *understand* why she did what she did. "If I could understand it, I could change it," she insisted, and I didn't agree.

I could appreciate that her mind was a great source of security and protection for her. I could see that unless she did understand something logically, she would never trust it or commit to it. But I was also certain that the complex patterns of anger defied simple, logical analysis. They required specific, rigorous, consistently applied Emotion Modification™ how-to's.

This client adamantly wanted to understand how her behavior patterns had accumulated. So I drew diagrams and described step by step how anger turns into rage. She also insisted that whatever the explanation was, her family was to be found absolutely blameless. She had a strong, defiant need for this to be "her problem."

To help her understand *and* not blame her parents, I explained it this way. "The people you know as your parents now are not the people who were in your life 15 or 17 years ago when you were a tiny child. At that time, your dad was away on active duty for months at a time. Your mother was left alone with three small children. She had been abruptly moved overseas, away from the support of her large, close extended family. The childcare and parenting support she wanted and needed from her family were absent. She didn't like military life. Neither did your dad, at that time. Your brother had severe asthma that required an inordinate amount of attention. You undoubtedly needed more time with both of your parents than you received. It was difficult for you. It was difficult for your mother. It was certainly difficult for your little brother. And also for your older sister.

"We can say without question that everything unproductive in your life is not your parents' fault. They are good, loving parents. They have always done everything they could for you and your siblings. But that does not mean that you experienced the love you needed when you were small. The intensity of your anger indicates you did not. The fact that you have hit and abused your brother ever since he was an infant is an indication that you resented him then, and that pattern has never changed. The fact that you sometimes love your mother, and sometimes you feel like you hate her... that, too, is an indication of a lot of unresolved anger.

What Is the Truth?

"I won't be able to help you change all of this," I said frankly, "unless we can see the truth. The truth does not come with fault or blame. That's what anger seeks. Love never needs to blame. Love needs to heal a situation. Truth allows love to fill in the spaces that anger currently occupies. Only when we can see the truth of what you are angry about, can we see the truth of how to redirect those feelings of anger and transform them into love."

She said she would try that. At the same time, she also wanted credible, logical reasons for trusting why changing certain patterns in her life would allow the deep-seated emotional patterns to change as well. She also wanted to understand why changing emotional patterns would affect the sleep and the teeth grinding and the headaches. I described the interconnectedness of all these, too.

Step by step we made progress. She questioned and challenged. I explained and instructed. She doubted and resisted some more. I assured and came up with even smaller changes she could make. Every time she tried something new and it worked, she was reluctant to admit the progress, but the joy and hope inside her could not keep her from admitting she was greatly relieved at the changes already underway.

The job, the speeding tickets, the headaches and teeth grinding—everything improved. She has fewer boyfriends now. She is setting better boundaries and making better choices. She has not completely eliminated the verbal abuse, but she at least no longer allows it automatically. She has feelings now when someone is abusive to her, and she now has feelings when the abuse comes *from* her. This pattern is taking some time, but she is applying new principles that give her new competency and hope.

The significant results that we have already accomplished were based on truth and emotional integrity. This young woman was willing to see the truth of where her anger came from, and she was willing to see how it compromised her emotional integrity. She could understand that unless her emotions had integrity, she could not experience self-love. So long as her anger caused her to lash out and destroy, she could not love her self. And until she had a supply of love within, she would not be attrac**tive** to or attrac**ted** to others who also had self-love.

When children's anger is out of control, the integrity issue is that they have not expressed the truth of their feelings and needs for so long that uncontrolled anger is the consequence. Their uncontrolled emotions are not in integrity with other aspects of their being, as a result. Whether the behavior and "being" that Ritalin suppresses is worth the trade-off is a decision each family certainly must make individually and carefully. Consider, in the meantime, another of Dr. Breggin's insights:

> "The children who are being diagnosed (ADD/ADHD) often represent our most energetic, individualistic, and creative youngsters. They are the ones who require the extra attention that our schools and families often feel unable to provide. Our diagnoses and drugs are in effect pruning a generation of our children by medically subduing any who stand out in ways that test our patience and skills. As a result, we are permanently impairing and undermining many of the children who would otherwise grow up to take leadership positions in our society."[4]

If more effective ways of understanding and managing anger can help reduce the administration of Ritalin (and other drugs as well), that is certainly worth examining, for all the reasons discussed, plus one more: emotional maturity.

Emotional Maturity and the Indigo Child

As this book's *Transforming Anger Into Love*™ chapter describes, each of the four basic emotions has a purpose. Anger is the emotion which, if suppressed in early life, leads to progressive stages of emotional suppression and dysfunction. Suppressing *any* of the basic emotions restricts each emotion from fulfilling its purpose. Suppression also renders that emotional energy unavailable. Whether suppressed by the developing ego or by swallowing a potent pill, the purpose and potential of the targeted emotion are reduced. "But that's the point!" frustrated parents and children say. "The potential of those unmanageable emotions is too intimidating. That's where drugs can help."

And so I say, "I know." I've worked with children and families on both sides of this issue: those who have used the drug and those who have not. I also will say that the last zombie-like, twitching, blinking, blanked-out teenage intellect extraordinaire I encountered so resembled the souls who dwell in state-run institutions that he, too, inspired this book. He was the second "Sam" in the summer of 2002.

The main difference between this second Sam and some of the other clients and families I have known is that this Sam's affluent family had migrated from school to school and practitioner to practitioner, trying herbal remedies here, energy medicine there, reading books, buying supplements, searching the Internet, railing at the universe… and the good news was that he hadn't pointed a gun at his step dad or himself since his new psychiatrist had prescribed Ritalin. (Yes, as chapter one describes, over a single three-month period, I encountered two young men who had threatened to kill their fathers.)

As I offer the guidelines in this book, therefore, I do keep the whole spectrum of my work in mind. For some families I have worked with, Ritalin has been a godsend. For others, it has been a nightmare. I had one client whose teachers petitioned the school administrators to insist that she be given Ritalin, and so she was. For carpooling and other practical reasons, the family needed to keep her at that school. They felt they had no other choice. I also know a parent whose grade-school age child was such a challenge in the classroom that the teacher cut out the top and bottom of a huge cardboard box and placed it over the child during class. Would Ritalin have been a worse choice? Who's to know? It's an emboldening experience, birthing these children and the lessons and teachings they bring.

Knowing the short- and long-term consequences of suppressed emotions, I am concerned that, as challenging as some of these children's behavioral and emotional aspects can be, Ritalin and its counterparts contribute to their arrested emotional development in a manner we are not factoring sufficiently. I suggest that this emotional consequence is a side effect not sufficiently discussed in the administration of these drugs. Especially in connection with Indigo Children, their emotional health is an essential complement to their advanced intellectual and creative potential. To rob them of the functioning of their emotions by administering drugs rather than careful, competent Emotion Modification™ is, at times, a testament to our inadequacy, not theirs.

In addition, Indigo Children *require* emotional maturity and integration to fulfill their purpose and actualize their potential. Part of their purpose is to expand our capacities to lovingly, creatively respond to their needs. Perhaps the best our love and creativity can do at some times for some children *is* to drug them. But too often, for too many children, drugs are given too soon and with too little consideration to the consequences of suppressing their emotional development and maturity.

Suppress vs. Express

"Between the ages of five to fifteen—the period of time when most Ritalin is prescribed—the brain undergoes new and striking changes in its function and even composition. Frequently used nerve pathways are firmed up while others are allowed to disappear from lack of use. There is a pruning back of up to 40% of the brain connections (synapses) in the frontal lobes of the brain—the part that most fully expresses human nature and human ability. Moreover, as described in chapter 1, new research discloses that the adolescent and young adult brain goes through yet another burst of growth and development....

Once a child begins to take a medication that changes his or her brain, it becomes nearly impossible to differentiate drug effects from other causes of the child's evolving or worsening difficulties.

Peter R. Breggin, M.D.[5]

For purposes of examining emotional maturity and the Indigo Child, the consequences of long-term suppression of emotions in *any* manner are relevant. This is particularly true for the drug-induced consequences of emotional suppression. Those consequences have not been adequately studied. They have not been compassionately and competently factored in the overall treatment plan. The consequences also have not been credibly incorporated in parents' guidelines. And finally, parents often are not given adequate information and support for anticipating and managing the after-effects of drug-induced emotion suppression.

Because the targeted behavior problems that cause parents to seek drugs are largely anger- (more accurately, rage-) related, the guidelines throughout this book will help. They do address the emotional buildup and consequences that long-term suppression creates. In the chapter on *Transforming Anger Into Love*™, the long-term development of patterns, as well as the reversal of such patterns, is addressed. In the process, long-term does not necessarily mean over the span of many years, or decades. A four-year-old who has had "behavior problems" since age two has already spent half a lifetime in the experience of that condition. Given the importance of those critical developmental years, it is likely that the patterns building during that time will be perpetuated, as the preceding quote from Dr. Breggin makes clear.

It is important to keep in mind, therefore, that anger is the first and principal suppressed emotion. Anger also appropriates other emotions into its patterns as the continually suppressed anger gathers momentum. Although anger-based patterns are not the sole contributor to emotional suppression, the power of suppression is progressive. It starts with anger, stops at nothing, and eventually creates the destructive condition of rage.

The long-term suppression of anger is the development that most restricts the capacity for emotional maturity. That emotion so arrested ceases integration and maturation the instant it is denied. What it does thereafter is need, and demand, and sulk, and plot how it can get attention and action. Not openly, and not appropriately, and in no way complementary to the adult struggling to carry on with part of its emotional power in twisted mettle. In age-appropriate accordance with the immaturity at which it is sequestered, the suspended emotion churns within. The adult matures, the physical and mental bodies mature, other emotions mature, and this left-behind emotion has no function but to continually exert itself in an effort to be noticed and included.

Such suppression can sabotage impressively. At times, however, there are developmentally healthy reasons for children to suppress their emotions. Sometimes they are afraid to say what they feel for fear of consequences. Sometimes they don't even know what they feel, or they feel vulnerable in the presence of a new or powerful emotion and they don't want that vulnerability to show. These are ordinary developmental moments of emotional growth and maturity.

The difference between such developmental rites of passage and the development of automatic, unproductive patterns of suppression, however, is huge. And so are the long-term effects. One leads to emotional exploration and identity, to emotional power and integration. The other leads to a variety of manifestations of a single outcome: emotional dysfunction and its direct manifestations.

Emotional Lockup

The patterns that build up to ensure automatic suppression are very powerful. They have to be in order for certain emotions automatically to be *sup*pressed rather than expressed. The patterns also constitute an enormous amount of emotional energy: the energy of whatever emotion is being suppressed, plus the energy required to *keep* that emotion suppressed. This is perhaps the most critical factor contributing to emotional immaturity.

A substantial portion of the children's emotional potential is locked up in these suppressive patterns. All of that emotional energy must remain so, in order to preserve the patterns that must be available instantly to serve the need to suppress. In addition, as the children develop new emotional options, those too are suppressed, and additional potential for emotional maturity is foreclosed. The original emotion is suppressed, the developmentally expansive emotional options are suppressed, and considerable energy is required to *keep* the emotions suppressed. All of this claims critical emotional potential.

When the suppression mechanisms can no longer hold the emotions at bay, the children suffering from these patterns often lose control, both emotionally and behaviorally. They don't plan to, and don't want to, but they can't help it. The foregoing describes a lot of energy that children must hold down every moment of the day without specifically concentrating on doing so. Children at this developmental age can hold down or hold back only so much. Then, those powerful energies break through. Their power exceeds the children's suppressive capability.

This is not a model for emotional integration or emotional maturity. It creates erratic patterns of emotional development. Even if drugs like Ritalin are suppressing emotional development, and even if drugs like Ritalin successfully erect a barricade to keep these suppressed emotions at bay, the emotions are unable to integrate with and complement the other (intellectual and physical, for example) aspects of the child that are maturing.

We do not know what the consequences of this artificially arrested emotional development will produce. We do know, however, the consequences that apply to elders who have suppressive systems in operation. We know from experience what happens when we ourselves have considerable emotional potential allocated into suppressive patterns. If we become tired or stressed or anxious or worried, our already limited available emotional energy is suddenly required to respond to these new developments, as well. At those moments, something has to give. That is when the suppression mechanisms crumble and yield, letting out the old, toxic, non-matured emotional energy stored inside us.

Given its unceasing efforts to be noticed and heard, that immature emotion gremlin sees the opening as soon as our suppression mechanism starts to shred and bam! Out comes one of those feelings we thought we'd buried. It's the worse timing possible and the worst way possible to say what our mature self had hidden and our immature emotional self now reveals.

"But we can apologize and explain and patch things up," we elders might suggest about those times. If we're emotionally healthy and have the emotional power and capacity to do so, apologizing can work. But if we're that healthy, we usually have the emotional integrity and maturity to function differently from the beginning of such emotional dilemmas. Therefore, if a considerable amount of our emotional power and capacity is allocated into these suppressive patterns, we may instead default into the suppressive options described in *Conditions of Emotional Dysfunction*. In that event, although we do apologize and explain every time this happens, our patterns continually repeat... including with our children.

For example, we may say to our young child, "This weekend we can go to the park and play." And on that Tuesday, it seems we will have the time and energy and inclination to go to the park. But workdays and life stressors being what they are, by the weekend, we may not have it in us to go the park. We may earnestly require a break. This is understandable on occasion. But we sometimes develop a pattern of not keeping our word. Our emotional capacities are unable to support our intentions and needs. Our matured adult self has certain standards that our emotional maturity cannot sustain. We say, "I'm sorry. I won't do that again." But we do. We do it again because of unmatured emotional capacities, and because of suppressed patterns re-engaged.

Emotional Immaturity, Needs, and Co-Dependency

Emotional immaturity is the result of unexpressed emotions held back by suppression. Perhaps we attempted to express the emotions in early life, but because circumstances did not allow or support doing so, the emotions were denied expression and integration. Because suppression originates with anger, the emotions were undoubtedly connected with needs. Suppressed anger is certainly always connected with needs. If the anger was suppressed, the needs were not met. As a result, those needs do not mature. The needs continue to assert themselves in a variety of subtle ways, however, sabotaging competent, well-intentioned adults' aspirations and self-esteem. Unmatured needs also often become unrealistic needs. They can be the driving force for unproductive, unfulfilling patterns repeated over and over.

The following is an example. It describes a parent whose unmet and unmatured emotional needs were carried forth into her daughter's life with continuing consequences. In this situation, the mother's co-dependency was as strong as her capacity for denial. Despite experiencing consistent feedback that her behavior was counterproductive and, at times, unwelcome, she nevertheless pursued her own needs in the name of her daughter. This mother's own needs were not being met in her marriage. She had given up a dynamic career to be at home with her "super child," as the parents referred to their daughter. The mother's bond with her daughter had all the indicators and implications of, "I want you to have all the things I didn't, and, I want to be the one who gets them for you."

This mother pushed her daughter to achieve in school, to excel in sports, to dress fashionably, to be popular, and to know what she wanted to "do" so that her school courses and preparation could be "correct." The daughter eventually rebelled. She hated school. She went from being adored by the teachers to the teachers becoming defiant about even having this student in their classrooms. As a last resort, the teachers collectively recommended through the guidance counselor that this young woman be given Ritalin.

All the while, the mother's aggravating presence at the school accomplished the opposite of what she insisted she desired. Her own needs and self-image battered school officials constantly with, "I'm doing everything I can to give this gifted child the opportunities she deserves (*i.e.*, I never had), and she doesn't even appreciate it (*i.e.*, no one appreciates me). She yells at me and treats me horribly. She plays her father against me. She tries to turn my own friends against me by enlisting their sympathies." All of this was unfolding as the classic presence and perpetuation of emotional immaturity.

Perhaps the mother was unaware that her own life did not meet her needs. Or, perhaps she was aware and simply did not know what to do as a result. Either way, the mother's patterns sabotaged the daughter's knowing what *she* needed, and finding the support *she* needed. In addition, the daughter felt guilty about not meeting her mother's needs and expectations, while at the same time resenting her mother's needs and expectations. In particular, the daughter resented that the mother found fault with whatever program or professional the family found to support the daughter's independence and individuality. The mother would promptly pull the plug on any intervention when it showed signs of competing with the daughter's need for the mother. And vice versa.

That the daughter's anger was escalating and ruining everything from friendships to her state of mind was not surprising. The child could not sleep. Her anxiety was so high that taking a test at school was hysteria producing. She called her mother from her cell phone at least a dozen times every day to experience some sense of connection. With each call, however, the daughter would re-experience her mother's inability to meet her needs. The daughter would inevitably hang up abruptly and angrily, and then call back, and hang up angrily again, and then call back.

The enactment of this pattern over and over again was an indication of the emotions, and the emotional adequacy, long suppressed. The daughter's needs were painfully unmanageable, her mother was painfully inadequate, and the emotional maturity to elevate them from these patterns was painfully absent.

Until the mother's needs and anger could be reworked, she lacked the emotional maturity to fulfill the contract she appeared to have with her daughter's future and well-being. Despite making so many efforts in her child's behalf, the mother's own needs and "behalf" were a constant underlying, intervening variable. The intensity of this mother's unmet needs was so much greater than her capacity to meet her daughter's needs that this condition continually compromised the mother's intended outcome.

One of the reasons that insights into these types of dynamics are relevant is that when we, the elders, try to help our children without being mindful of these types of patterns, we often contribute to the grids that anger-based patterns create. When we re-enact the same patterns over and over again with our children, anger is the cause. It is the principal emotion that locks repetitive behaviors and restrictive outcomes in place.

Love is the creative emotion. It either creates a positive outcome or it creates the space to attract a positive outcome. When we feel ourselves locked into rigid, unproductive patterns, identifying some way to address our own suppressed anger is essential. It is the key to unleashing additional emotional power and potential. Our adequacy to assist our children in addressing their suppressed anger is often derived from our own capacity to do the same.

Grid(un)Lock™

Nancy Tappe, who first saw and announced the Indigo Children, says they are going to be "more head than heart."[1] They still require emotional balance and integration, however, principally because the actualization of their gifts and potential require those qualities. In addition, these children know that their emotional self must be aligned with and supportive of their exceptional gifts. Indigo Children, therefore, regret and resent when the emotional conditioning they are experiencing does not complement their gifts. They often prod and prompt us to expand our own emotional adequacies because they need us to model more adequacy for them.

As Indigo Children mature physically and intellectually, spiritually and psychologically, and yet certain emotional potential and capacity are arrested, an imbalance results. The children's emotional needs cannot be met if those needs are not included and integrated in the children's over-all repertoire. This is important because of the anger-based patterns that often develop among Indigo Children. Many times they are sweet, sensitive, adorable, loving little Beings whose anger issues seem to develop almost overnight.

Parents are shocked. They often say, "This isn't the child I knew. Where did this come from? What did we do?" With Indigo Children, it is easy to be so absorbed with their gifted aspects that we often ignore their developmental emotional needs. However, if these children do not learn how to recognize and honor those emotional needs, and how to navigate the world in a manner that meets those needs, the emotional consequences that result will be anger based. And unfortunate.

The reason is that anger is our automatic emotional response when our needs are not met. The purposefully disruptive energy of anger is designed to be expressed into the situation that does *not* meet our needs, and disrupt or reorganize that situation so that it does meet our needs. Then, because love is our automatic emotional response when our needs *are* met, our experience of love is expanded, as is our emotional competency and confidence.

Therefore, if anger is suppressed—and especially if an automatic pattern of suppressing anger is developed—the arrested emotional development that results can create long-term unproductive patterns. The anger is suppressed, the needs are not met, and the children do not experience love in the manner that the connection between human needs and emotions allows.

These developments unfold if children's emotional needs are not recognized. They also unfold if the children are not taught how to experience their needs being met by negotiating with the outer world in a manner that allows those needs to be met. Imagine, then, how we endanger these children's essential needs/emotions development if the children's needs and emotional capacities are restricted and suppressed with drugs like Ritalin.

Unconnected to the True Self

As authors Carroll and Tober say about Ritalin:

"Here is a sobering thought: If you are a parent with a sedated child, you might feel that Ritalin is a real solution. The child behaves better, seems calmer, and things are more stable in the family and at school—whew! Ritalin, however, puts the child into a holding pattern of behavior—which the child may even like. But later in life, when the stopper comes out of the bottle (when they come off the drug), the bubbles inside may still cause some kind of explosion. In retrospect, after growing up, they may feel that they lost part of their childhood in a murky remembrance unconnected to their true self. Ritalin often postpones the real issue of growing up, and the wisdom that comes with it—learning how society works. This is documented."[1]

Part of the real issue of "growing up" and the real "wisdom" that Ritalin postpones is *emotional* wisdom and maturity, including learning how to utilize and rely on the dynamic, God-given emotion of anger. If that emotion is suppressed and manipulated to a severe degree, the consequences are not only debilitating. They can also be destructive.

We already know that self-induced suppression mechanisms cause anger to build into rage. We know that rage can be externalized as volatile outbursts, or internalized, as depression, fitness or work obsession, eating disorders, and chronic illnesses. When rage is the reason parents turn to Ritalin, the child already has a problem with suppressed anger. To be effective in a whole-person sense, therefore, the automatic pattern of suppressing anger must be addressed in concert with the Ritalin. Otherwise, the effects of self- *or* drug-induced suppression can produce outcomes in the Indigo adult like the ones described next.

This Is What I Need

Children who suppress anger—or who are given medication that suppresses anger—do not learn to recognize or utilize anger as an indication of needs. This means that certain needs of the developing child or young adult are likely to be unrecognized, unaddressed, and unmet. The nature of needs, however, is that the primary, primal needs will continue to assert so that they *are* met.

Imagine, for example, a child whose early-life need to be recognized in relation to a sibling is never met. Many children go through such a stage and yet learn ways for that need to be met through recognition in school, or athletics, or creative expression. In that event, the evolution of the unmet childhood need is successful, and no long-term problem ensues. If the need does not evolve successfully, however, or if the child does not outgrow that need, then the need does not mature. It remains an unmet need and, since anger is our automatic emotional response when our needs are not met, the anger from that unmet need lingers. Suppressed, but lingering, the energy from the need pulsates.

"I need recognition!" it silently screams. So the child acts out and is a behavior problem. Regardless of what the teachers or coaches or peers do, it's never enough. Whatever the need is, it is insatiable. Many efforts by many competent, caring people are still inadequate under the circumstances. The child's behaviors persist despite changing schools or neighborhoods or martial arts instructors or therapists.

In these instances, the need is trapped at a stage of *emotional* development that does not complement the child's developmental age or developmental skills in other areas. Therefore, with Indigo Children, the changes we logically would identify may be especially counterproductive. Changing schools removes them from the location, but the unmet needs change locations, too. The excitement (or relief) of a new school and teachers and peers can bring a temporary respite from the troublesome patterns the unmet needs create. But if the same patterns emerge again, this indicates underlying, unaddressed, suppressed emotional needs that will not be resolved by finding a new school or a new drug.

To add to the challenge, this needs-based condition usually is evident in more than one arena. In the example of the unmet-therefore-perpetuated need for recognition, the need can come out in a competitive sport. The child is too attached to winning, to excelling, to being perfect, and to being praised. A child with this condition often is unable to praise or support others, or to lose gracefully. The child is the last to be chosen by others, because the child's needs clash with the environment of team effort, cooperation, and sharing.

In adulthood, this individual may advance in a career, marry and have children, and become a community leader, but the emotional maturity factor can still sabotage on a regular basis. Needing to be accepted by "the guys" can lead to drinking after work. A lot. Needing attention by dressing to a certain standard can be obsessive. And excessive on the pocketbook. Taking things too personally can lead to resentment by co-workers, so advancement in the company is withheld.

Later in life, emotional immaturity can result in emotional unavailability. A person whose own needs are not sufficiently met cannot be adequate or available in connection with meeting others' needs. Emotional immaturity is the reason a spouse or partner needs to control. Because emotional immaturity also spawns emotional insecurity, issues of jealousy and trust can plague a business or personal relationship unnecessarily, and unfairly.

Emotional immaturity often results in emotional inadequacy as a parent. "Being right" and "doing it my way" are indicators of inadequacy if they become patterns and themes in one's parenting style. If punishment and control are the parent's only choices, this indicates the parent lacks the emotional adequacy to negotiate, or to set and model emotional boundaries. The parent is more adequate at enforcing rules than in bonding with the child.

For Indigo Children, this can be extremely limiting, and painful. They are explorers and adventurers in the emotional realms. They can take us elders to places we've never envisioned in relation to emotional depth and joy. It is heartbreaking for them when we reach a limit that our own emotional immaturity imposes. It is equally painful for us not to experience the gift that their emotional intelligence and presence can bring.

So Many Colors in the Rainbow

> *Flowers are red, young man.*
> *Green leaves are green.*
> *There's no need to see flowers any other way*
> *Than the way they always have been seen.*
>
> *Flowers Are Red*[6]
> By Harry Chapin

In this song that expresses the experiences of so many Indigo Children, Harry Chapin tells of the little boy whose teacher makes him color all flowers red. "But," the little boy says… "there are so many colors in the rainbow, so many colors in the mornin' sun, so many colors in a flower, and I see every one."

"Well," the teacher said, "you're sassy. There's ways that things should be done. And you'll paint flowers the way the way I say," and she put him in a corner saying, "It's for your own good. And you won't come out 'til you get it right… responding like you *should*."

After a while, the little boy changes schools, where the new teacher smiles and says, "Painting should be fun. There are so many colors in a flower, so let's use every one." But the little boy paints flowers in neat rows of green and red. And when the teacher asks him why, like the plaintive melody in the background of this song, he says:

Flowers are red.
Green leaves are green.
There's no need to see flowers any other way
Than the way they always have been seen.

The Gift of Indigo Children

They are
Our greatest gift
Our greatest challenge

Our greatest teachers

and

Our greatest hope.

Let us therefore call forth
In all space and time

The Truth of
Who they are
What they know
What they feel
What they need
and
What they are here to do.

So BE It.

Notes

Chapter Ten

Homeopathy and How It Can Help

An Interview With
Melanie Melvin, Ph.D. – Psychotherapist and Homeopath

Melanie Melvin, Ph.D., DHM, RSHom, CCH, has a doctorate in psychology and was licensed in California from 1988 to 1996, and from 2000 to the present. She is also licensed in Colorado since 1994, but is currently practicing in California. Melanie has a diploma in homeopathy, is a Fellow of the British Institute of Homeopathy, is a member of the North American Society of Homeopaths, and is certified by the Counsel for Homeopathic Certification. She has been combining homeopathy and psychotherapy/counseling with her clients, including children, since 1980.

Her information is included in this book for many reasons. Her comments in Carroll and Tober's first book, *The Indigo Children*, were profoundly insightful and helpful, and I especially appreciate her saying in that book:

From Melanie Melvin, Therapist:

"The angriest children I have seen… are those without parental limits. I have witnessed children push their parents to anger just so the parents would set limits on the children's behavior. You are abdicating your role as a parent if you allow your children to control you."

From Melanie Melvin, Parent:

In addition, Melanie, who also is a mother, writes of a time when her young son was testing her. He kept touching something on the coffee table, and she kept smacking his fingers. "He was in tears," she writes, "and my heart was breaking, but I knew that if I gave in he would be more deeply harmed. It would mean that he had beaten the parent, who was supposed to be bigger, stronger, and more dependable, and able to keep him safe—*and that is frightening for a child*! After that incident, we hugged; he was happy and never needed to go to that extreme again. If I had given in, we would have had to repeat that scenario many, many times until learning the lesson to be strong, not overly sympathetic, and aware of the bigger picture.

"When there is a pattern of defiance in an Indigo Child, it is usually because they feel disrespected or feel that you are not respecting yourself by giving your power away to them… If you truly love your children and are not looking to them to fill your needs to be loved and accepted, the highest good for all concerned will be served."

From Melanie Melvin, Homeopath:

"The difference between acute and chronic homeopathic remedies is that acute remedies available in a health food store are for temporary conditions—injuries, colds, flu, headache, etc. A person's condition is considered a *constitutional* problem if there is a weakness that is leading to repeated injuries, headaches, colds, etc. This means there is a chronic weakness leading to frequent symptoms or illnesses."

A Note About Homeopathy:

As you will read, the homeopathic remedies Melanie discusses in this interview have been extremely effective and beneficial to Indigo Children and families. I have personally benefited from homeopathy for decades, and have referred clients for homeopathic treatment since 1981. Because homeopathy is a practice of deep understanding and treatment of conditions, it is important to distinguish between homeopathic remedies available from the health food store for acute conditions, and those available from a homeopath for chronic conditions. For the chronic conditions addressed in this book, it is important that Indigo Children and families seek the counsel of a licensed homeopath.

To find a homeopath in your area, you may wish to contact the organizations listed in the Resources section at the end of this book.

From An Interview with Dr. Melanie Melvin

The Importance of Treating Indigo Children with Respect

Dianne: In your work as a therapist and homeopath, what have you experienced as the challenges with Indigo Children and their families?

Melanie: What is so crucial is that these children are treated with respect. They come in with more self-respect than previous generations, such as their parents and grandparents. We did not have the degree of self-respect they have. We were taught to put ourselves down and not see ourselves as valuable. To think too much of ourselves meant we had a "swollen head," which meant we were conceited, or were selfish. Our generations have had to struggle to gain some sense of self-worth. These kids have more of a sense of who they are. Therefore, the most crucial thing you can do for these children is to look into their eyes, one spiritual being to another, and to feel respect, one heart to another.

I don't suggest talking to them like they are adults. But, look them in the eye, and talk to them with respect. You can make things clear in their own language or in ways they can understand, but the important point is that you actually *feel* respect for them. They know when you do not. And that is, I think, where the anger comes from.

D: Please elaborate on that.

M: To know you are a valuable spiritual being (as, actually, all of us are), and to be regarded as if you are JUST a kid without much to offer, is an affront. No wonder they want to figuratively or literally put up their dukes! I view anger as the emotion that is triggered when we feel trod upon. It is like a warning signal inside us that says, "Stand up for yourself," when we feel that we are being used, or our self-respect and free will are being trampled.

That is what the anger is about with these children. They feel they have to stand up for themselves because they are not being respected, and they get angry because they can't get through to the parents or the teachers who often treat them in a manner that is condescending. Such as, "You're a little kid. You can't think for yourself. You just have to do as you're told." That does not work with these children. And in fact, it really *shouldn't* work, with any children or adults. We all deserve respect.

Listen and Hear Their Information

D: What can you say that will help parents and teachers who may be interacting with their children in this manner, and experiencing unproductive outcomes?

M: They need to listen to the children. If there is a problem in the family, or in school, then they need to have a discussion—parents and/or teachers *and* students—and ask the kids, "What's going on?" in referring to a particular behavior. And ask them, "What would work better? What are *you* thinking? How can we (which *includes them* in the process) solve this problem?

Approach a situation with them just as you would with a respected adult, and not by treating them as bad children, which is what frequently happens. Often these kids come up with better solutions than we can if we listen to them, because they know what is bothering them. They know what would work, and what they need.

We need to listen more. After we have listened, it is then appropriate for us to share what we see and feel, which solutions we can agree with or not, tweaking the solution until everyone can live with it. Try it, and come back to tweak it again if it's not fully working. Always remember to acknowledge everyone's efforts and attempts at solving the problem! Appreciation and gratitude to all involved is nectar for the heart and soul!

Being an Indigo Parent

D: What has been your own experience as a parent of two Indigo Children?

M: I was the oldest of six kids, with five brothers, and I had a great deal to do in helping to raise the others, so it was my natural tendency to be respectful, to get along with children, to listen to them, and to treat them as equal. Therefore, it was a natural experience for me to relate to two Indigo Children... although I didn't realize they were Indigos until they were teenagers.

Indigo Children as Clients

D: Is that when you realized some of the children who were clients in your practice were similar to your children?

M: Yes and No. Let me say first that I think there have been different groups of Indigos (now adults) who have been coming to Earth periodically, for many years, to test the waters. It was an experiment to see what worked and what didn't as far as raising the vibrations of the human race. My kids are now 22 and 24, so they were some of the early Indigos in one of the more recent waves.

Because of how I was raised and the experiences of my life, as well as what I brought into this life as a spiritual being, I already respected others' rights, whether they were child or adult. I knew that the principles I used with my own children were needed with all children. What I observed was that Indigos, including my own, were less likely to put up with disrespectful treatment. And I don't mean that *they* were disrespectful. Their interactions were as one Being talking to another Being. I could see that, and I knew that was what these children needed. They needed to be treated with dignity, asked their opinions, and invited to participate in creative solutions.

They also needed to be empathized with, and honored when they had criticisms of the status quo. For example: having so much homework after school. The amount of schoolwork and extra curricular activities is an unbalanced way to live. They come home from eight hours of school and they're asked to do four hours of homework. That would be like our coming home from work and also having four hours of work to do in addition to everything else.

Or they are rushed around to so many activities, there is no down time for anyone—parents or children. Therefore, some of the children's complaints are very legitimate. They know that this is out of balance. We need to honestly acknowledge when they are right, rather than defend the established way of doing things.

Parents of Indigo Children

D: As you realized the nature of the children who were your clients, what were some of the challenges and attitudes you encountered among the parents?

M: Frustration, anger and impatience, and a desire to have the children listen without questioning... because that is how the adults were raised. Also, a lot of times the parents wanted me to "fix" the kids, so that they were "more manageable." It was also interesting to discover—I guess because of the nature of the world—that quite a few Indigos have come to parents who are not at all "aware" that their children are not like they were as kids. These children are a new wave of human, and it is the job of the parents to teach principles and values—such as integrity and the golden rule—not rules for the sake of rules, and blind obedience. If you expect blind obedience from these children, you are in for some butting of heads!

Ideally, our goal is to raise responsible, self-actualizing adults, not so-called "good" children... if that means not thinking for oneself and simply doing what one is told. How can they change things for the better if they are too accommodating or easily intimidated by those in authority?! If nurtured and guided, these children are the future adults who will change the world. Help them become all they can be so they can do the best possible job!

Treatment and Symptoms

D: How do you utilize homeopathy with these children, and with these types of situations?

M: What I look at is their whole symptom picture. And try to figure out what the core issue is.

D: What are some examples of the core issues that you have encountered?

M: A lot of Indigo Children need the Nosodes, which are types of remedies. They treat hereditary influences that are in the family. For a long time, the majority of remedies I used with these children were the Nosodes, and the primary ones were Tuberculinum, Medorrhinum, and Carcinosin

Remedies for Indigo Children

D: What are some of the remedies you find effective for Indigo Children and their families?

M: Homeopaths speak of remedies as if they are personalities, because remedies do have personalities. For example, a Pulsatilla (which means someone who is needing Pulsatilla) is very dependent, needy, clingy, and soft emotionally. This is not typically a remedy an Indigo would need because these children are not that way. They are much more strong-willed and independent. Contrast Pulsatilla with Anacardium, a very angry, aggressive remedy. Indigos are more likely to need Anacardium or another strong-willed remedy, rather than one that is mild and yielding. Anacardium is an angry remedy. A remedy for angry people. They are angry and can be violent.

D: Anacardium is an angry, aggressive remedy?

M: Yes. In addition, underneath Anacardium's anger is low self-worth. What happens with some Indigos is that they start out life pretty confident of who they are, and then they are treated consistently as though they are "bad." Other kids don't want to be around them, the teachers think they are "bad," the parents think they are "bad," and pretty soon their self-worth starts to go down.

But, they are strong enough people that they are angry about it. They don't just crawl into a hole and conclude they're no good. They are angry and they want to fight back.

D: Does Anacardium help them gather that angry energy and direct it appropriately?

M: Yes. Instead of hitting and beating and attacking, they begin to feel their self-worth, and they stand up for themselves in a way that is more effective. They are not acting out to the point where their teachers and parents just feel like they're "bad." They have more effective ways of asserting themselves.

D: For example?

M: For example, this one little boy was actually hitting his mother a lot. He was also acting out at school—getting into fights—so I gave him Anacardium and he started to reduce the amount of acting out at school. He began to learn how to get along with other kids better. He stopped hitting his mom, and now he talks to her about things. He tells her how he feels, and what he thinks, and what he wants. Now, when she disagrees with him, he'll discuss it with her rather than starting to hit her.

Remedies for Parents

D: Are there remedies you also give parents to assist them?

M: If I can figure out what their constitutional remedy is. For example, his particular mother was Magnesium Muriaticum. The Magnesiums, as a family of remedies, can't stand violence, so she was intimidated by him. When she started taking her remedy, she began standing up for herself better. As a result, the two of them were meeting each other more like equals. Instead of her being afraid and cowering, which made him angrier, she started coming across as stronger: being a mother, and setting limits that were appropriate, and being less afraid of him. All of these allowed him to feel better about himself.

When you react to someone as if they are frightening, you insinuate they're a "bad" person because only "bad," scary people are frightening. This implication makes them angry.

Remedies for Fear of Anger

D: Is there a remedy that works with the fear of anger?

M: Yes, there are certain remedies that are "more angry," and there are certain remedies that are "afraid of anger."

Like the Magnesiums. Magnesium Muhr, Magnesium Carb, Magnesium Sulf, Magnesium Phosporic—all the Magnesium remedies. They are all for people who have a lot of trouble with anger;

people who can't stand violence in any form. Also, Staphysagria is another one for people who suppress all of their own anger, so they also don't like anyone else getting angry.

All of those remedies are for fear of anger—their own, and, other people's anger. Another comment about fear is that it often is the other side of the coin from anger.

If I put myself in an Indigo's shoes, and I've come to this planet because I know I have a job to do, then I'm going to be anxious, agitated, and very frustrated if I feel like I can't get through to the adults in my world to let me do what I came here to do. The road is not easy if you are dealing with people who do not understand what you're trying to communicate.

What Indigo Children Need

D: I know that one of the reasons for these children's anger is that they know if they lack the emotional integration and maturity to match or integrate with their gifts and potential, then those gifts and potential, and even their purpose, will be compromised and sabotaged. Perhaps even thwarted. Therefore, one of the messages that these children give us very intensely is that their emotional needs or dysfunction are a hidden message that says, and demonstrates for other to see, "This is the condition I need help in resolving and re-organizing, because so much is at stake if I don't."

M: Yes. Their symptoms, their anger, and acting out—these are an outcry from the spirit. These children's spirits won't let them fade away. They need to stand out because their purpose needs to be addressed and honored.

I often believe that when the children come to me, the vital force or the spiritual aspect of them is letting me know exactly what needs to be addressed so that I can give them a remedy (and maybe some respect, recognition, spiritual love) that will help them heal. Then they can leave my office and get back on their path.

D: From your perspective as a therapist and homeopath, would you say that these children are giving the same message to the parents, but you happen to be able to interpret it and act on it?

M: Yes. And that, maybe, their giving the message to the parents was enough to get the parents to bring them for help. Then I can hear what they are saying, and try to attend to what they need.

Sadness and Hyperactivity

D: My own approach to anger and emotional dysfunction works with the interaction of four primary emotions: love, anger, fear, and sadness. I understand the tie-in between fear and anger you have discussed. I also teach that when someone's anger develops into the condition of rage, there is a relationship between the rage and sadness.

M: Definitely. I'm glad you brought this up because, with the children who are hyperactive, the hyperactivity usually includes some anger and acting out. When the hyperactivity starts to reduce, you'll find sadness and/or low energy or depression underneath.

That unfolded beautifully with this one little girl who needed Tuberculinum. She was four years old, and she had the whole Montessori school, including the teachers, intimidated. The neighbors around the school were calling to say, "What are you doing to that little girl? We can hear her screaming." We gave her one dose of Tuberculinum and they called me the next day. They wanted to know what I had done, because she totally turned around. She needed maybe one or two other doses over the next year.

After she calmed down like that, her mother confided in me that she, too, used to throw those same kinds of tantrums, where she would look in the mirror to see if she was giving a good enough performance. That definitely speaks to the hereditary factor.

Then, after a few months of her not intimidating everybody, this profound sadness came out: the feeling that nobody liked her, that she wasn't accepted, nobody wanted her around… she just felt sad, and almost depressed.

Both low energy and sadness are often underneath hyperactivity. Hyperactive kids are often revving themselves up to overcome low energy. It is not that they are so active naturally. They are overcompensating for not having enough energy, or for feeling sad or depressed.

Indigo Children's Purpose

D: My own sense of these children's role in connection with healing the anger is that they, and those in their families who also have difficulty with anger, will eventually find the information and tools and practitioners to transform their own anger, and thereby contribute to the body of information available for the masses.

M: Yes. I agree. And I think it's interesting that so many substances are being "proven" in homeopathy. A "proving" is the way that homeopaths find out what symptoms a substance will heal. The plant, animal or mineral substance is given to a relatively healthy individual in diluted, potentized form, and the symptoms that the individual develops teach us what that remedy will cure in a sick person.

If the sick person has the symptoms of a particular remedy, then we know to give that remedy to help the person heal. "Like cures like." That is why we must match the symptoms of a sick person to the symptoms covered by a particular remedy. That is also why one needs a homeopath in more constitutional or chronic care—it takes skill to find the exact remedy out of more than 2,000 homeopathic remedies.

Substances being proven in homeopathy now, include the milk of the cow, and the sheep, and the horse, and the lion, and the cat. They are all being evaluated as to what symptoms they cause and, therefore, can heal. All of the milk remedies have to do with nurturing, love and bonding—which are too often lacking in the modern family where both parents work and mother returns to work soon after having her child. These separations cause breaks in the bonds of connection that all the family members need.

I think we need to understand the consciousness of every life form on the planet in order for all of us to expand our consciousness. We expand and increase our vibration by including and incorporating an understanding of the consciousness of everything. This is part of becoming one with everything. For example, when we prove the milk of the cat, we can begin to understand the consciousness of the cat. The cat milk is diluted and shaken in order to become a homeopathic remedy. It is then given to human "provers" to experience the symptoms—and also the consciousness of that animal, the cat.

In the proving process for the milk of the cat, the provers began to feel that they had to prostitute themselves in order to be fed and cared for. Yet, they resented having to compromise their sense of independence. When we look into the history of the cat, we find that the cat is the only animal that voluntarily domesticated itself. It gave up independence in order not to starve. Apparently, at that time in Egypt, it was likely to starve if it stayed in the wild. Putting ourselves in their paws, we might feel resentful having to compromise our independence. We might periodically lash out (scratch, bite) at our "captors." And at other times, deign to let them pet us when it suits us. Proving the milk of the cat helps us understand the consciousness of that being. It seems that the consciousness of the cat is stuck in the dilemma of independence vs. dependence.

Every plant, animal, mineral, element, etc., has a consciousness. As we take these into ourselves in the form of a proving with each plant, animal, mineral, and element on Earth, we increase our compassion, empathy, and ability to be one with all that exists in this world. We also begin to heal wherever consciousness is "stuck" as we take the substance in and feel compassion and love toward that being and toward that same dilemma in us.

As we heal ourselves, it changes the consciousness of the planet and the universe. The Indigos are part of changing the pattern of the global consciousness.

~ ~ ~ ~ ~

Contact information:
Melanie Melvin, Ph.D.
13328 Granite Creek Road
San Diego, CA 92128
(858) 513-9293
Cmelwolf@aol.com

Chapter Eleven

Emotions, Energy and the Body:
A Guide to Symbology,
Meaning and Understanding

Symbology and the Indigo Children

Among the words used to describe Indigo Children, "sensitive" is one that is used most often. Many Indigo Children are extremely sensitive—to feelings, sound, nature, creatures, and colors. With their exceptional intuitive abilities, they are also sensitive to others' thoughts and feelings. For these reasons, this interpretive information on symbology is included in this book. It will help the elders in these children's lives be more attuned to the subtleties of these children's experiences of life. This information will also help the children interpret and better understand some of their own actions.

In the last portions of this chapter, there are guidelines for understanding the ways Indigo Children use and absorb the energy of the items and resources in their lives. For example, when they say they need a new comforter or a new backpack, trust them. If at all possible, help them obtain replacements for those items as soon as possible. And let them do the selecting.

"But there's nothing wrong with the bedding he has *now*!" I recall an exasperated, financially challenged single mom insisting. With no younger child to pass her son's bedding on to, and no inclination to give it to a charity, she was bordering on refusal. Her child's manipulative talents were legendary in their family. This mother had been battling with the child for years. At this point, she was not at all eager to replace perfectly good bedding with different perfectly good bedding. It didn't make sense. It had to be his way of manipulating her again.

Only when I said, "It's my idea, not his," did she listen. And only when I explained why did she begin to realize that the idea could be connected to her child's sleep disorder. His current bedding was red and black. It was appealing for his age group. His friends liked it a lot. I was confident, however, that being surrounded throughout the night with the pulsating energy of red interfered with his ability to rest. The sheets were not the only factor, certainly. But they were contributing to his sleeplessness.

My suggestion was blue. The lighter and softer, the better. A blue-to-lilac pastel would have been my first choice but I knew not to go for that. It was a stretch for either of them to think that natural fibers, like cotton, would make a difference. ("They're much more expensive," the mother had complained, understandably.) So I made only a brief comment about energy flow and synthetics, and hoped for the best. After a few weeks, the mother did take her son shopping for new bedding. He found a teal color that was acceptable. (A combination of blue and green. Good start!) I never asked about the fiber or thread count.

I will say, however, that these subtleties matter with Indigo Children. A lot. How these children's physical surroundings absorb energy is very significant. The objects in their lives often have special and specific meaning and purpose. It is important that we honor the value, function, and purpose that these children ascribe to these objects. Along these lines, I often suggest that Indigo Children explore writing with a fountain pen, including those with calligraphy points. The soft flow and unique feel of these pens can be soothing and expressive. The colors and shapes of the pens, the selection of points (fine, medium, broad, italic), and the variety of inks are often very appealing. As the *Identifying Hidden Symptoms of Anger*™ chapter denotes, pressing heavily when we write is an indication of anger (pent-up emotional energy) stored in the body. Changing a child's writing instruments can help the child become more aware of certain emotional energy and needs, rather than leaving that information to come out indirectly in the writing behavior.

The symbology and significance of Indigo Children's relationships with their pets are also extremely important. Many of us have known for a long time that pets often absorb the energy of humans' emotional distress. Pets' illnesses and injuries are often those creatures' valiant efforts in that regard. Because Indigo Children often bond with pets in this manner, it is important for us to honor and trust these children's needs for the pets and creatures in their lives. They offer immense comfort, and a quality of connection that Indigo Children often need.

This includes not only domestic, but wild creatures, as well. It may be implausible for the family to travel cross-country for the migration of Sand Hill Cranes or the laying of sea turtles' eggs, but these children have a keen awareness of the ecological and environmental patterns and developments. Whatever the family can do to support an Indigo Child's interest in nature and wild creatures is important for reasons many of us may not understand.

Aspects of these children that are not honored and not fulfilled may eventually show up as anger. If their anger is suppressed, it may result in additional emotions being suppressed. In the instance of suppression, those emotional energies are often exiled into the body. In this book that is filled with indicators and information about emotional energy—both suppressed and expressed—the information in this chapter offers especially useful insights into the role of the body as a storehouse of unexpressed emotions. Some of the following Body Postures are widely known as reliable communications from the body.

Body Postures

Since body language and body symbology are a lot alike, many of us are already familiar with these body-centered communications:

Folding our arms against our chest: Creates a barrier between us and the other person.

Leaning closer: Indicates interest, and trust.

Leaning away: Indicates needing distance – from the person or from the subject matter.

| **Avoiding eye contact:** | Indicates lack of self-confidence; not trustworthy. |
| **Hands in pockets:** | Indicates resistance; withholding. |

For centuries, Eastern Medicine, acupuncture, and other healing modalities and systems have utilized even deeper communication from the body. They are based on the relationship between emotional energy stored in the body and the advent of significant physical symptoms, messages, and dis-ease. This chapter is about further communications from the body: how the body indicates the presence of suppressed emotional energy, and how the body attempts to release that emotional energy in a variety of ways.

The body's cells, muscles, organs, and other systems were not designed to store emotional energy. But when emotions well up inside us and we do not express or absorb their energy emotionally, that energy has to go somewhere. The descriptions in this chapter depict where unexpressed emotional energy resides in the body. The information also describes how subconscious thoughts are associated with that emotional energy as it is activated within the body or released from it.

The purpose of this information is to contribute in a meaningful way to the Indigo Children and the communications they are conveying. These insights will enable us to be more responsive and sensitive to the messages these children are giving. They will also help the children understand the emotional messages their bodies reveal.

Subconscious Associations

To benefit most from the information in this chapter, it will help to learn the different areas of the body that store different types of suppressed emotional energy. It will also help to learn to pay attention to the thoughts or feelings in the subconscious that occur simultaneously with the gestures to those areas. They both go together.

As the first example of the subconscious patterns associated with body symbology, we will use the gesture for chastisement. The top of the hand is where suppressed energy from feeling chastised is stored. Sometimes that part of our hand will actually itch. But often, we stroke or scratch that part of the body without even being aware of the gesture.

We are also likely to be unaware of the thought or memory that is passing through our subconscious at the time of the gesture. Whatever we are thinking or feeling at that moment is what activates the gesture. If suppressed energy of feeling chastised in the past is stored in our body, it is because those feelings from being chastised in the past were not expressed at the time we experienced them.

The Symbology of Physical Pain

Physical pain is related to emotional pain that was too great, or too painful, to experience at the time it came up; therefore, we exiled it into the body. We store that painful emotional energy in the body and later *feel* it in the form of physical pain because the body is used to host that pain.

A good example is the instance of breaking our little finger. That is where emotional vulnerability is stored. The finger breaks due to the intensity of so much energy being stored up for so long that it finally had to be released. The finger can absorb and hold only so much. If we could instantly identify what we were thinking at the moment of breaking our finger, that subconscious information would be a clue about the type of energy being released. For example, we may have been thinking about our job, or about some friction in the family. Either one could result in our feeling emotionally vulnerable.

Prior to the break, it is likely that finger gave us a number of messages. All of the messages were attempts by our subconscious to break up the automatic, emotion-suppressing patterns that were causing energy to build up in the body. The patterns were engaging, the messages were multiplying, and we were so regularly disregarding them that the finger went "snap." The emotional vulnerability we were feeling, but avoiding, accumulated to such a degree that an actual break was eventually required to release that emotional buildup.

The symbology of the break is twofold: That degree of pain needing to be released requires the break. And also, that type of "space" is required for that much intense energy to finally exit the body. Even if one of the previous warning signs was a hangnail on that finger, the symbology would be the same. The *degree and intensity* of energy built up and creating only a hangnail is substantially less than a break. However, the *type* of energy (emotional vulnerability) is the same.

Maybe a month ago we noticed a hangnail on the little finger. If we knew symbology, we knew the hangnail was a message about emotional vulnerability. At that time, the hangnail was only slightly painful. That meant there was still time to pay attention to the subconscious thoughts and get *their* message before the body had to break a bone.

At that time, we could have thought, "What am I feeling vulnerable about?" If we didn't get the answer at the moment, we would know to monitor our subconscious. Somewhere there would be a clue. But since these clues often go flitting by, we may have missed the next clue, as well. The paper cut. And the next one, too: a jammed knuckle. All these would have been on the same finger, perhaps over the period of a month. If the energy is really building, though, we could experience two or three of these kinds of clues in a day.

The problem is, we often do not notice them. We are too preoccupied. Or, if we do notice them, we don't honor their message. Consequently, the body keeps generating the messages, we keep ignoring them, and the body gets more and more creative trying to get our attention. If we ignore enough messages enough times, the outcome requires even more intense messages. In this instance, for example, when we require a trip to the emergency room.

Look at the symbology of going to the "emergency" room, and all of that intense drama. If a young couple is there with their baby, it's not a coincidence. It's all part of the symbology. Our pattern of emotional vulnerability no doubt started in infancy. At least, that is the likely meaning of the presence of the couple we watch for two hours while we wait for the emergency room staff to tend to us. Perhaps we notice how devoted and concerned they are. Or, perhaps we notice that they are not very attentive at all. As we pay attention to them, whether consciously or otherwise, it is likely we are experiencing or re-living some early-life patterns connected to feeling emotionally vulnerable.

Taking this symbology another step, look at the attention we will receive from a number of people at that emergency room. That scenario could also coincide with the origin of our emotional vulnerability: we were neglected. Now we create an environment where our vulnerability is attended, ideally, with compassion and competency.

Look also at the splint or cast that will be required, along with the inconvenience of having to maneuver with the finger bandaged and stretched out for weeks. All of this indicates there was a lot of energy related to emotional vulnerability stored in that little finger. The degree of the pain we experience is proportional to the emotional pain of the original (and even subsequently felt and suppressed) emotional vulnerability. All of the circumstances of the emergency room, including how we got there (did a friend or loved one drive us, or did we go alone?), are symbolic and meaningful in connection with our patterns of suppressing emotional vulnerability.

Introduction to Body Symbology

The foregoing is an example of how many messages can be combined into a single body-centered event. The following will add even more to our understanding of the symbology of body communication.

When I first began to accumulate and apply and verify this information, I had no idea there was other teaching along these lines that represented body symbology differently. It was a real surprise to me, therefore, when I discovered that almost universally the left side is considered the feminine, receptive side of the body, and the right side is viewed as masculine, transmitting. Now I realize that there are many energy systems in the body. They all serve a purpose. They all offer insightful, valuable information. Each of us finds the right information at the right time to assist us in expanding our awareness for whatever our needs and challenges are at that time.

The information in this chapter is specifically about the consequences of suppressed anger. This information also pertains to the anger-related patterns that deflect emotional energy into the body when anger and the emotions compromised by it are not expressed. For this body of information, therefore, a symbolic communication from the right side of the body is, in general, a message about the feminine presence in our life. Depending on our own gender, if we are feminine, we look first to our self, then to the feminine parent or principal feminine presence in early life. Next, we look outward, to the current relationships with the feminine gender. It is important to recognize that this applies to the feminine aspect of a male as well, since this information applies to the feminine principle rather than just to the feminine gender.

The same principles stated above for the feminine apply to the masculine. If the body communicates from the left side, and we are masculine, we pay attention to what we were thinking and feeling at that moment, looking first to whether the message is about us. If not, we apply the message to the masculine parent or principal male/s influencing us in early life; then to the male/s currently in our lives. A female with body communications on her left side would look first to the principal male relationship/s in her life, then to male/s in early life; then to male/s in her environment (such as co-workers and neighbors).

We look first to our self because what *we* are doing or thinking or feeling is most often what has activated this energy within the body. However, the patterns of suppressing emotional energy frequently originated in early life. As we grow and mature and evolve, we gain the capacity for releasing that unproductive energy. It is always helpful to look at the early-life environment if we are unable to identify which events in our current life are related to the body's messages. These emotions are stored in layers. Eventually, we will release enough of the layers to get to the original cause. Then we can heal.

Hair: The Samson Legacy

Too Short

Hair is about power, as the Biblical story recounts. Samson's physical strength and power were legendary. He knew the source of that strength and the power he had as a result. He also knew not to reveal the source. When he did, he lost both the strength and the power. In these more contemporary times, when we arrange for someone to cut our hair, we usually describe how much we want cut, where we want it cut, or where we do not want it cut. If that person cuts off (takes away) more than we have asked for or agreed to, that transaction indicates we are giving up our power in some way at that time in our life.

Because humanity's source of power is truth, we can know from that transaction to look at our relationship with truth, although that can be a very complex task. Giving up our power certainly relates to being inauthentic in some way. But as the emotional integrity issues throughout this book discuss, the very fact that we have suppressed emotions means we were not honest about what we felt or needed at the time. It is not surprising, then, that from time to time, a haircut jolts us into feeling anger. Anger is our emotional response when our needs are not met, and it certainly does not meet our needs for someone to take more of our hair than we have given them permission to take. Ideally that anger will enable us to identify how we are giving up our power in a relationship or situation, or even in relation to a pervasive subconscious pattern.

As all the symbology systems suggest, the layers and layers of emotions we have suppressed or even completely lost touch with all have meaning. It is our task to pay attention to the information that comes into our awareness from these suppressed emotions, even though their messages may be fleeting. By paying attention, we can eventually gain sufficient insights to transform the automatic patterns produced as a result of these automatically suppressed emotions. Hair does grow back. Whatever truth we are avoiding will return.

Too Long

It is also possible to allow our hair to be too long. In a way, "too long" is completely subjective; but as the Indigo Essence section in this book indicates, each of us does have our own set of standards. What is too long for one person is not necessarily too long for another. What matters is whether we follow the intuitive nudges that suggest we get our hair cut, or that we allow it to grow.

If we are feeling powerless in our life, we may choose to let our hair grow as a result. We may be trying to obtain some sense of power by having more hair. However, not only will that not work; it will even be counterproductive. Because the truth registers at all times, the truth of why we have let our hair grow will emanate from our hair whether others consciously get that message or not. We can go for a job interview and think our hair looks great—and maybe it does—but if we are feeling needy and dependent and powerless at that time, our long hair will reflect that.

We might get the job. We might even get the job because the interviewer likes our hair and our overall presentation. But as our tenure at that company unfolds, we will discover there is a culture there of enmeshed, co-dependent dynamics. We will have been a perfect fit at the time we interviewed because that is the condition we were in, and of all the candidates for that job, we fit best with the co-dependent culture.

Too Controlled

One last point about haircuts—the regularly scheduled ones. It is important to examine the routine of all fixed appointments, and especially the ones for automatically having our hair cut, say, every six weeks. Maintaining that routine may be appropriate, but only if each time the six-week period comes up, we ask ourselves whether it is time to have a haircut or not.

Body Symbology

The Symbology of Ears

Ears are indicators of what we are hearing, whether or not we are listening, and our subconscious response as a result. For example, gestures to the ears indicate our subconscious response to what we are hearing. If we pull on or stroke our earlobes, it means we are straining to understand what we are hearing. If our finger goes into our ear canal to scratch it, we really don't like what we are hearing. The deeper or longer or more energetically we scratch, the more energy we are exerting to express how much we do not like what we are hearing. We are trying to clear out the hearing channel in hopes of hearing differently, or even blocking out hearing the words as they come.

Large earlobes often signify that a person is a good listener, while practically no earlobes can signify a person is not a good listener.

Earaches signify the pain of what we have been hearing for so long that the ears now ache from absorbing those conversations, or that information. The painful energy accumulates because we do not respond. Perhaps we do not feel we have the permission, or the courage, or even the capacity to express our feelings and to halt our being subjected to those words that are causing such pain. Earaches are not only about what we are hearing on the outside. They can also result from what we are hearing on the inside from the thoughts and patterns we self-generate. For example, we may repeat to ourselves, "If you don't get good grades, you'll never get into college," or "You'll never get a good job," or "You'll never amount to anything." If we get an earache at, say, age 15, it could be related to hurtful words we have heard; then we replay the words over and over in our own mind; and finally we release the pain from those words—but in the instance of an earache, we release the pain physically, not emotionally.

The Symbology of the Forehead

This is the area of the body where worry is indicated. When we stroke our forehead, it indicates we are trying to generate new thoughts or solutions to something that is worrisome.

The Pent-up Energy of Headaches

They, too, can signify worry—accumulated to the degree that it is painful. In essence, headaches are about anger-related tension. Usually, however, if the anger has been suppressed for so long that it has accumulated to produce a headache, the headache indicates we are far removed from the original source of the anger.

Migraine headaches are the extreme example. Western Medicine, as well as Eastern, has all types of diagnostic explanations for them. The explanations all make sense to the extent that they physiologically explain what is going on in the body that accounts for the physical pain. But if medicine understood the cause underneath—the cause that impacts the capillaries and blood flow and other body functions that result in migraines—then medicine would also have an answer for helping people with anger. The patterns of suppressed emotions that create migraines start early in life. While there are undoubtedly associations between migraines and the types of stress in the environment that activate the migraines, there also are associations with the onset of migraines and the types of stress and emotional pain suffered in early life. The nature of patterns produced by suppressed emotions is that those patterns continue to attract and co-create similar situations. Therefore, the migraines continue.

Migraines from changes in the seasons may have originated when it was fall and we didn't like school. Maybe we were dyslexic, and no one knew it, so the pressure of learning and studying and having to stay at home when the other kids were outside all combined to give us a big headache. If our parents were unsympathetic, that may have made the pain worse. Since we still don't have the support and nurturing we need in our life, the migraines continue to say that.

The Symbology of the Eyebrows

Eyebrows are basically designed to keep perspiration from draining into the eyes. Perspiration is usually the result of exertion. Or heat. Heat can symbolize anger. Exertion can be the result of over-doing because our anger kept us from acting on the signal that we needed to stop. Or, since anger is the emotion of excess, stored-up anger can be the suppressed emotional force that drives us to over-do. Love is the emotion that seeks and creates balance. *Anything* excessive and out of balance is the product of anger and not love.

Stroking the eyebrows means we are activating that part of the body that protects something from coming into the eyes. The brows are close to the forehead, which symbolizes worry. Stroking them can symbolize an effort to erect some kind of barrier to what we are seeing. Stroking the brows can coincide with conversation or contemplation that results in our seeing something that is worrisome. Or, the energy activated in the brow area can indicate that the information we are getting is not clear.

Much of the symbolic information stored in the body requires interpretation. The eyebrows are an example. They are part of the protection of the most significant of our five senses: sight. On the other hand, we also have the sixth sense sight: intuition. Therefore, gestures associated with the brows can indicate a response to what we are seeing with either seeing source. With all the symbology contained in this chapter, whatever is occurring in our subconscious mind must be incorporated in the full understanding and application of this information.

The Symbology of the Eyes

The areas around the eyes are where sadness is symbolized. Tears fall from three different places in the eye. Tears fall from the outside of the eye when we feel out of control in connection with what we are crying about. Tears falling alongside the nose signify we are sad but we feel we can deal with the sadness. The third place tears fall is from the center of the eye. That area signifies we are in between: we are not feeling out of control, but we are not feeling very confident either. Sometimes the first tear falls from one side and one area; then a tear falls from the other eye. And in the course of a good cry, the tears can fall from different areas. They can even fall differently from one side than from the other. If we pay attention to our thoughts as we cry, we will understand these indicators.

Gestures around the eyes also denote sadness. For example, if someone makes a gesture to his or her eye, it could mean that whatever is being said, what they are hearing or thinking as a result, it is activating their sadness.

When considering the symbology of the eyes, it is also significant to think of the age-old saying, "An eye for an eye, a tooth for a tooth." Originally, that contrast was about proportionality. "An eye for an eye, *but* a tooth for a tooth." In other words, the eye is a significant organ. There are only two eyes, and if one is damaged, the person is dramatically affected. On the other hand, there are 32 teeth. If one is damaged, the loss is considerably less in comparison.

The Symbology of the Nose

Scratching our nose is an indication of anger. It means we do not like what we are thinking or what we are hearing. This is demonstrated most energetically when we rub our index finger back and forth in the area of our nostrils to signify our anger.

Sneezes also are anger. If a person had been honest about the emotional impact of what we were saying (*e.g.*, this is making me angry), the suppressed emotional energy would not have necessitated the sneeze. As it is, the suppressed emotional energy is too much to hold in. Given that the sneeze breaks up the train of thought, it may cause the conversation to be directed differently. At that point, the anger has indirectly served its purpose: it has produced change.

The Symbology of the Mouth and Lips

Since the stomach is the organ of assimilation, and food originates its journey to the stomach by way of the lips, gestures to the lips can be about assimilation. We may purse our lips or roll our tongue around inside our mouth because we are experiencing difficulty assimilating information. In some form, this difficulty is causing us to feel some degree of anger.

Lips also are an indication of our style of emotional expression. Our style of expressing anger, especially. If the line defining the top lip flows upward *gradually* from the area at the corner of the mouth where outer definition of the lips begins—and if it then rises gradually to the center of the lips underneath the nose—this signifies a person who expresses emotions evenly. This person is even-tempered with anger that is slow to rise. This is contrasted with the outer part of the lip line, starting at the corners, being almost concealed. Then the lip line abruptly shows. This is an indication that the person has an inclination to hold back what they are feeling or wanting to say. Then it finally comes out. This indicates someone who is inclined to suppress anger, then (possibly) explode.

An excessive number of lines and creases in the lip area usually signifies someone who talks a lot.

Ulcers in the mouth, canker sores, fever blisters, and "accidentally" biting the tongue or inside of the jaw indicate energy coming out from stored-up anger. The anger is related to what we were thinking or feeling when we first notice, or experience, these indicators.

The Symbology of the Teeth

Teeth are one of the principal areas in the body where anger is stored. Clenched teeth, grinding teeth, toothaches, tooth decay, and gum inflammation are all related to anger. The diagrams in this chapter indicate the ages in which baby and permanent teeth appear. The suppressed anger stored in the body at the time those teeth came in is held in the teeth thereafter.

It is helpful when addressing conditions affecting your teeth to know at what age the teeth came in. You can review what your life was like at that time, what anger your teeth have stored as a result, and what you are doing in your life now to neutralize and replace those energies. Or, you may be perpetuating a similar pattern now. Cavities, fillings replaced, crowns, root canals, extractions… they are all indicators of anger the teeth have absorbed that you may now be releasing, or replacing. If we elect to have our mercury fillings replaced, symbolically we have emotionally matured sufficiently to "go into" that anger and replace it according to our growth and development as an adult. We may consciously choose to do so based on the toxicity of mercury fillings, but it is actually the toxicity of the original, built-up anger that we are seeking to replace.

Any such attention to our teeth can have that impact and meaning. A root canal can mean that a tooth has absorbed all the pain it possibly can for now. Its contribution has gotten to the root of the anger accumulated from a particular age, and now that root is used up. It may not have to be extracted, however. When that is necessary, an actual hole must be created to let out all the energy stored inside. The symbology of a crown is similar. Much of the tooth has been used up to accommodate the stored-up anger, but a new "covering" has been created by the mature adult as a result of that person's emotional growth.

Cavities and fillings are necessary to drill into the stored-up anger. It is eating away from the inside. "Outside influences" in the individual's life—family, support systems, financial security, etc.—all are inadequate to absorb and transform the anger. Therefore, the degeneration must be stopped by someone on the outside.

By learning the connection of suppressed anger stored in the teeth, when we go to the dentist's office, we can anticipate and prepare for the release of the anger. In addition, we can obtain the symbolic message from the anger and participate in releasing it in the most healing manner possible. We can thank the tooth for its role in absorbing the anger we were unable to express, and we can be thankful that our own emotional growth and maturity have allowed that suppressed anger to be accessed and released.

If we are unable to be grateful for the dental appointment that releases anger—if instead we are afraid of dental appointments—there are two possible factors connected with that fear. One is that we are afraid of our anger, and we are afraid to connect to the suppressed anger being released through the dental procedure. The other dental fear factor is that our teeth are so sensitized by the amount of suppressed anger they have absorbed, we fear we can't accommodate any more trauma connected to the emotional energy the teeth already are storing.

If we neglect flossing, changing toothbrushes regularly, having our teeth cleaned regularly, and other dental hygiene routines, that neglect is the product of anger. We may know to floss, and we may know that our dental bills would be considerably less if we did floss. So we buy floss, and put it in a prominent place, but still, we don't floss. Why? Anger from our own experience of neglect. It blocks us, still. And its toll on our teeth is great.

The Symbology of the Jaw

This area of the body is where knockout blows are delivered. If we stroke our chin or beard, it can be a form of contemplation. It also indicates that what we are thinking or what we have just said or heard has dealt us a blow.

The Symbology of the Throat

The throat area of the body is where air (breath of life) can be cut off. It is where strangulation occurs. Therefore, gesturing to the throat signifies fear. Whatever we are thinking about, hearing, feeling, or saying feels like it has a stranglehold on us in some way and is causing us to be afraid. For example, coughs signify fear. As this book outlines in the preceding chapters, suppressed anger can cause us to develop certain types of fear.

The Symbology of the Shoulders, Neck, and Back

Shoulders symbolically carry "the weight of the world." Pain across the shoulders is specifically related to our feeling burdened. Pain in the back, around the shoulder blades, activates the feeling of being stabbed in the back. It is the result of our feeling that someone is not being honest with us or has betrayed us.

Inability to turn our neck signifies having focused in a certain rigid way for so long that we have lost sight of alternatives, especially those that might be available in the outside world. We feel like we have to do everything ourselves, and that limited thinking limits our seeing other options. Stiff neck often indicates that we are not including others in our solutions. We blame ourselves and feel we are the sole solution. In this process, we become rigid, and the range of motion in our neck signifies that.

Lower back pain is about unexpressed emotions in relationships: intimate ones, most likely. Depending on our connection with other family members, friends, co-workers, or neighbors, lower back pain *can* be related to them. It is usually someone close, however, and usually someone whom we would refer to as our being in a relationship with.

The Symbology of the Lungs

The lungs store sadness. Smoking is based on the need to cover up sadness. In addition, someone gesturing to that area of the body is indicating that what they are hearing or thinking is connecting them with sadness. The habit of shallow breathing and holding one's breath is due to the sadness that causes a person's lungs to feel, and sometimes actually be, compressed or collapsed. The sadness is so great that the person doesn't energetically embrace, reach for, or take in deep, full breaths of life.

Holding our breath can also extend from fear. However, as various topics in this book explain, stored-up sadness is connected to a buildup of fear. The sadness is about inadequate love. The fear is also about inadequate love. As the patterns related to inadequate love begin to accumulate, each has a different function. The chapter on *Transforming Anger Into Love*™ outlines this progression in detail.

The Symbology of the Kidneys

The kidneys store fear. As a major filtering system for the body, the kidneys also take on the assignment of filtering suppressed fear that the person has been unable to express or release. Alcoholism takes a toll on both the kidneys and the liver (and skin and other functions of the body and psyche, as well). For purposes of this symbology section, alcoholism is the product of the fear that results from the anger that blocks a person's relationship with love. Excessive drinking is, therefore, an effort to suppress fear.

The Symbology of the Liver

The liver is also a major filtering organ in the body. In addition, the liver takes on the assignment of filtering suppressed anger the person has been unable to express or release. Drugs take a toll on both the kidneys and the liver (and other functions of the body and psyche, as well). For purposes of this symbology section, drug addiction is the product of the anger that blocks a person's relationship with love. Drugs are, therefore, an effort to suppress anger.

"Is this true for over-the-counter and prescription drugs, or marijuana, cocaine, methamphetamines, and such?" you might ask. Keep in mind that some people consider alcohol and nicotine drugs that happen to be legal. "So what is the symbology of *drugs*?" Needless to say, because anger is a complex emotion, so are the consequences of suppressing it. For purposes of anger, the harder the drugs, the harder the formation and deeper the damage of the anger the drugs are trying to medicate or avoid.

The pharmaceutical industry serves humanity in significant ways by creating compounds that alleviate the consequences of emotional dysfunction. Until we have dominion over our emotions, we benefit from its products—over-the-counter and prescription. Likewise, if there were sufficient love in our lives, we would not be addicted to any substance or habit. Until our experience of love is so, the needs and choices for recreational drugs reflect the inadequacy of our relationship with love, principally, self-love.

The Symbology of the Arms

As the traditional fight / flight symbology suggests, arms are another primary area of the body where anger is stored. Upper arms are closer to the body than forearms. An incident affecting the upper arms is likely to be about "us." The forearms signify anger related to individuals or situations in the outer world.

The Symbology of the Legs

As the traditional fight / flight symbology suggests, legs are another primary area of the body where fear is stored. Thighs are closer to the body than calves. Something affecting the thigh is more likely related to "us." Calves are related more to fear connected to individuals or situations in the outer world.

The Symbology of the Hands

As discussed in the introduction of this chapter, scratching the tops of the hands symbolizes chastisement. Recalling the image of a child being hit on the top of the hands with a ruler connects us to this symbology. The chastisement gesture signifies being criticized and punished by an authority figure. When someone gestures to this area or receives a scratch, a burn, a blow, or a bruise, the symbology is related to excessive punishment, ridicule, chastisement, and cruelty. At the moment someone gestures to that area of the hand, the person is feeling, or is reminded of, chastisement. In later life, that accumulation of suppressed emotional energy shows as age spots.

The Symbology of the Finger Tips

The tips of the fingers are a gathering place for particularly sensitive nerve endings. Therefore, we are particularly sensitive at the ends of our fingertips. People who have really long nails—especially people who glue really long nails onto their fingers—are, in general, signifying that they are feeling extremely sensitive to something or someone in their life. They are trying to protect their sensitivity with those long nails.

A blow to the fingertip, such as hitting your fingernail with a hammer, signifies some form of anger that is, or is bordering on, self-contempt. The very fact that you hit your "self" means you are angry with your self. In addition, blood accumulation is anger. The nails are designed to protect that sensitive part of the finger. Therefore, the symbology of this action is that you are hammering and injuring your own self-protection. Or, you may be angry because you do not feel you are protecting or defending yourself from something or someone.

The Symbology of Joints

In general, joints are about flexibility. The upper body is related to anger; the lower body is related to fear. The joint closest to you is about self; the mid-range joint is about people close to you; the joint farthest from you is about people in the outside world. Therefore:

This joint	is	anger toward:
• **Shoulders**	=	Self.
• **Elbows**	=	People close to us.
• **Wrists**	=	People/situations in the outside world.
• **Hips**	=	Self.
• **Knees**	=	People close to us.
• **Ankles**	=	People/situations in the outside world.

As additional information, the knees are part of our body's maneuvering mechanisms. Our knees assist us in navigating the outer world, away from what is constricting or threatening us (lower body is fear).

Knees, therefore, absorb the energy of feeling vulnerable due to our emotional patterns. Knees keep us from removing ourselves from a constricting, possibly even threatening-to-our-emotional-well-being situation.

If we are feminine, and the right knee hurts or gets injured, we may be unable to free ourselves from obligations we feel toward our mother, or a mother figure, or a female authority figure. The left knee could be similar vulnerability felt in connection with the father, or a father figure, or a male authority figure. The energy stored in the knees could also be related to others in the family, co-workers, neighbors, etc.,—anyone whose impact on our emotional well-being is causing us to feel vulnerable and to feel that we are unable to free ourselves from the situation.

Achilles Heel: Although not a joint per se, this area of the body is about extreme vulnerability. Something that "hits us" at that level and area of vulnerability can wipe us out or bring us down. In addition, it takes quite a lot of maneuvering to accomplish an injury, a blow, a bruise, or a scratch to that area. We must pay careful attention to a thought at the time we are hit in that area—or at the time when we, for example, jam that area of our heel against the base of a chair. If we are planning something at that moment, whatever we are feeling or needing from that plan warrants extra attention.

The Symbology of Fingers and Toes

Remember: The right side is the feminine, and the left is the masculine. The information related to joints also applies to the hands and toes. The joint closest to the body is about self; the middle joint is about people close to us; and the farthest joint is about people or situations in the outside world.

Little finger and little toe	=	Emotional vulnerability.
Ring finger and third toe	=	Relationships.
Middle finger and middle toe	=	Sexuality.
Index finger and first toe	=	Career.
Thumb and big toe	=	Direction in life.

Additional Body Communications

Stubbing your toe, getting a hangnail, breaking a fingernail, breaking a dish, dropping your keys, the phone line going "dead" in the midst of a phone conversation, scratches, cuts, bruises, accidentally hitting yourself, or someone hitting you—these types of incidents are all significant. Attracting a poisonous insect to penetrate your skin and inject venom is a *really* dramatic attempt on your body's part to get your attention so that you will release some pent-up anger.

Biting is anger. Nail biting, especially. This even applies to an infant who is learning how all of its body parts function. If the infant accidentally bites us, that infant is letting us know he/she is angry about something.

Excessive pressure is anger, including pressing too hard when writing. Gripping the steering wheel can be fear, but because pressure is anger, look there first. (It may be both. You're angry, you're running late, and you're afraid of the consequences.)

Red Hot = Anger

Anything hot or red is connected to anger. This includes anger being discharged from the body in the form of acne, bleeding, fevers, inflammation, infection, blisters, cuts, and burns. A sty on the eye represents anger that is coming out as sadness. Fever blisters also are anger coming out of the body. Other types of blisters, on the hands or feet, for example, also represent anger. If the blisters "pop" on their own without our being aware of their doing so, that represents stored up anger from neglect. To have gotten the blister in the first place is another likely aspect of neglect. We did not cease a certain activity that was painful and abusive to our body.

Car overheating, leaving the stove on, burning dinner, running the bathwater too hot… these are the product of anger-based thoughts preoccupying us to the extent that we do not pay attention.

As this chapter emphasizes, it is always important to pay attention to what you were thinking at the time that you, for example, bump into a table and bruise your right thigh. Knowing that the thigh represents fear, if you are a man, bumping your right thigh would signify the feminine. Was your thought or feeling about the feminine aspect of yourself? Your sensitivity or vulnerability, perhaps? (Thigh is closer to the body than the calf, so it is likely a message about self.) Or was your thought or feeling about a female in your life? Your mother? A female co-worker? By applying the entire spectrum of information in this chapter, you will soon learn what your body and body messages are conveying to you.

The Symbology of All Colors

For Indigo Children especially, their selection of colors and preference for colors can be very important to them. In addition, this information can be revealing and helpful for the parents. In general, these children will non-consciously choose colors based on whether they are transmitting colors or receptive colors. It is important not to ascribe too much meaning to their color selections, however, since there are many reasons children choose their colors and clothing combinations and accessories. The following are a few simple guidelines that can be helpful for understanding your children's color-coded messages.

Red
Orange   These are the transmitting colors.
Yellow

Green   Is neutral. It neither transmits nor receives.

Blue
Indigo   These are the receiving colors.
Violet

Black   Lets in and absorbs everything.
           It is the least discriminating.

White   Lets in and absorbs nothing.
           It is the most discriminating.

Beige   Fear

Frequently Asked Questions about Symbology

Q: "But what about when things just itch? I didn't feel angry. My nose was just itching."

A: Certainly your nose was itching. And the reason it was itching is that there is anger-related energy stored in the body and it was trying to come out, so it caused you to scratch your nose. In addition, if you will take note, you will notice that that energy came out in a manner to scratch your nose precisely at the time you were thinking about or feeling about something connected to anger. As you learn to pay attention to the timing of these incidents and to the thoughts and feelings they accompany, soon you will get in touch with the feelings and thoughts they are connected to.

Q: "Are all sneezes, all the time, about anger?"

A: Yes. If not your own anger, then someone else's you are picking up on or reacting to. Before you conclude that this is too absurd, spend a while paying attention to the principles in this chapter. If they still feel incongruent with your belief system, trust that. This, like all interpretive information, is helpful to the right people at the right time. You may be learning about anger in ways that the sneeze symbology does not complement right now.

Anger-based patterns can be quite intractable. If new information illuminates the patterns, then those patterns have to reorganize in order to stay functional. Patterns in your life right now have undoubtedly served an important function for a very long time. They may have more service to provide in your life. Therefore, they will not want to be noticed every time you sneeze. They will need to be revealed and transformed more gradually. Trust that.

Timetable for Ages When Baby Teeth Are "In"

Here is an average timetable detailing when a child's primary (baby) teeth are "in." At this age, the upper part of the tooth has fully appeared through the gum.

For purposes of the symbology information in this chapter, use these ages as the period related to suppressed anger stored in the teeth.

Tooth	Age in Months
A. Second Molar	24
B. First Molar	14
C. Cuspid	18
D. Lateral Incisor	9
E. Central Incisor	7 1/2
F. Central Incisor	7 1/2
G. Lateral Incisor	9
H. Cuspid	18
I. First Molar	14
J. Second Molar	24
K. Second Molar	20
L. First Molar	12
M. Cuspid	16
N. Lateral Incisor	7
O. Central Incisor	6
P. Central Incisor	6
Q. Lateral Incisor	7
R. Cuspid	16
S. First Molar	12
T. Second Molar	20

Baby teeth

Timetable for Ages When Permanent Teeth Are "In"

Here is an average timetable detailing when a child's permanent teeth are "in." At this age, the upper part of the tooth has fully appeared through the gum.

For purposes of the symbology information in this chapter, use these ages as the period related to suppressed anger stored in the teeth. The ages listed are an average, mid-point timetable. The teeth may come in earlier in some children; later in others.

Tooth	Age in Years	Tooth	Age in Years
1. Third Molar	19 1/2	27. Cuspid	10
2. Second Molar	13	28. First Bicuspid	11 1/2
3. First Molar	7	29. Second Bicuspid	12
4. Second Bicuspid	11 1/2	30. First Molar	7
5. First Bicuspid	11	31. Second Molar	12 1/2
6. Cuspid	12	32. Third Molar	19 1/2
7. Lateral Incisor	9		
8. Central Incisor	8		
9. Central Incisor	8		
10. Lateral Incisor	9		
11. Cuspid	12		
12. First Bicuspid	11		
13. Second Bicuspid	11 1/2		
14. First Molar	7		
15. Second Molar	13		
16. Third Molar	19 1/2		
17. Third Molar	19 1/2		
18. Second Molar	12 1/2		
19. First Molar	7		
20. Second Bicuspid	12		
21. First Bicuspid	11 1/2		
22. Cuspid	10		
23. Lateral Incisor	8		
24. Central Incisor	7		
25. Central Incisor	7		
26. Lateral Incisor	8		

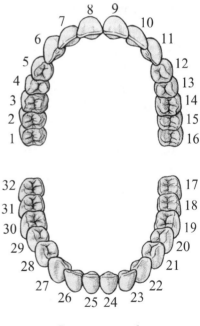

Permanent teeth

Notes

Chapter Twelve

Journal to the Anger:
Journey to the Love

A Healing Exercise for Everyone

An Overview of the Purpose and Potential of This Exercise

When anger is suppressed and allowed to accumulate into a reservoir of old anger, it can be difficult to reach. "How can reaching my anger be the problem if I already vent *too* much?" some people ask when I introduce this exercise. "And how can writing about it help? I need to *change* my anger, not get more in touch with it."

People who view anger this way are unaware of how anger-based patterns accumulate and then produce unintended consequences. To help our Indigo Children redirect the consequences of their anger, we must somehow get to the root of that anger, which is somewhere in the past. Often, these children are repeating behaviors both they and others agree need to stop. The children even say they are trying to stop their anger patterns, but they can't. This exercise can be especially beneficial for those children, and for the entire family.

If you have never journaled, it can be a powerful, enlightening exercise. Even if you have frequently journaled, this exercise will be a unique way to help identify and transform anger. Sometimes it is meaningful to select a particular writing pad, or a book of blank pages, or a notebook, or file folder. Some people even use a special pen for journaling. Each person's journaling style is different. In the "Whatever Works" portion of this exercise, you will find suggestions for how to help your children participate. If they are old enough to write, and inclined to write, help them with the supplies to do so. Otherwise, the examples in this chapter make clear: writing is only one way to create meaningful dialogue and agreements for changing the anger-based patterns. If you are inclined to participate in several ways, try them all!

For the writing exercise, it is important to have no rules. In fact, that is one of the benefits of journaling. It will reveal many of the restrictive patterns you may not realize affect your daily life. For example, journaling is a free-flowing, unedited, uncensored exercise. You let your pen do the talking. You might start with, "My anger is about…" or "The changes I would like to make with my anger are…" or "I don't know why I stay angry…" and let the words flow from there. If you try too hard, that is likely to be a pattern that this exercise will identify, and ideally, help you replace with self-acceptance. This is *your* exercise. No expectations. No arbitrary or self-imposed standards. No time frames. No rules about complete sentences or writing legibly. Journaling is about allowing your words and thoughts and feelings and memories and needs to flow.

Because this exercise is likely to lead to some new exchanges with you and your family members, it may help you identify your own anger-based patterns. Or, it may help you realize you are angry with others in your family and have not shared that anger. As you journal, you might feel that anger very intensely. By the time of the family meeting, however, you will have had time to consider how you want to express or report your anger in a loving manner.

Journaling to the Anger is an opportunity to identify and release anger on paper, or in the project you and your family create. Ultimately, however, you want to release the anger so that you can feel more love. As you journal about your anger, therefore—or perhaps, after you have journaled about your anger—reflect on how you can express your anger, or release it, or forgive others, in a loving manner. Reflect, also, on how your anger has taken a toll on your own experience of love. Reflect on your untapped potential to be loving. Look at ways your anger often keeps you from realizing that full potential for love. Consider discussing this with your family members. Let them hear that you want to be more loving. Ask them to help you when they do not experience you as loving. Ask them to help you be more mindful of and accountable for your anger. Ask them to help you recognize when your anger is unfair, or judgmental, or out of proportion.

Ask them to help you be loving even when you are expressing your anger, and your needs.

How This Exercise Can Help

One family who did this exercise together achieved wonderful results. In the beginning, they created an "altar" in their family room to signify the anger each one got in touch with through this journaling exercise. The agreement was that family members would represent their anger at this altar, and then discuss the anger in a manner that was healthy and loving. Their eldest daughter eventually dragged her twin-bed mattress to the altar. It seems that several months prior, her parents had agreed to get her a larger mattress. They had taken her to stores looking at headboards and mattresses a number of times; yet, she still was in her single bed. And she was angry.

The Indigo Child in the family was a bit more subtle. She put a dollar bill on the altar. Family members noticed it; they did not automatically know its significance; they also did not ask. That eventually was this child's point. She left the bill there for days, hoping someone would ask, "What's the message?"

"I give you [my family] all kinds of clues all the time about what I'm angry about and what I need," she finally said at a family meeting about the messages at the altar. "Dad keeps saying, 'I wish I had a dollar for every time you get angry.' Well, my message is, I wish I had a dollar for every time I tell you exactly what I want, or need—and you tell me you hear, and that you'll do what I've asked—and then days or weeks go by, and you don't. When I bring it up you say, 'We've had some unexpected bills. Or, take your turn. Or, we haven't had time.' But then Dad needs a new briefcase and you get *that*. Mom's hair color runs out and she spends a hundred dollars to cover the gray. You've completely redone the baby's room. And we have time to go to Granny's twice a month. But what about ME?"

You see, this journaling exercise can be a new and creative way to bring out the anger messages that regularly roar through these children's minds. In the family situation described above, both children agreed they constantly stayed angry because their parents did not keep their word. "I can live without a bigger bed," the eldest daughter admitted, "but I get sick of your excuses. They make me enraged." The Indigo Child made her position clear, as well. It was about trust. "You're always saying one thing and doing something else. Then you get angry with *me* because I bring that up."

It wasn't as if this family hadn't talked about these things before. They were recurring themes, in fact. And they produced recurring arguments. But when the words came out at those times, everyone was already activated and defensive, so nothing improved. One of the reasons this exercise works well is that the entire family journals. Then the family gathers in a meeting that is declared a neutral space. Instead of exchanging words when everyone's anger is already activated, which is often the pattern, the family discusses these matters when everyone has agreed to listen. This family bought a new mattress after their first meeting. It was a very powerful, loving experience, too. They also put a jar of pennies in the kitchen. It seems, trust and integrity and keeping one's word was a huge, unspoken issue among all family members.

To begin working through this issue, they gave one another a penny from the jar when one member felt the other had not been in integrity. They agreed not to discuss the issue at those times. They simply gave the penny, to signify there *was* an issue. They also agreed not to accuse or blame at those times. They were to only say why they were giving the penny. Then, at the family meeting, they would discuss these matters.

For example, when "Sue" gave "Beth" a penny, Sue said, simply, "You told me you would help rake leaves. I spent two hours. You helped for fifteen minutes. I don't feel that was in integrity." Beth was to accept Sue's statement without defending or explaining at that time. Those explanatory exchanges were to be deferred for the family meeting. The penny exchange was to be a simple, non-accusatory exchange. "This was my experience. This is why I feel it lacked integrity."

At the scheduled weekly meeting, the two family members with the most pennies were asked to talk about how they felt when the pennies were given to them. Those two family members also listened to what the others felt when these recipients' integrity had not been maintained. The two with the most pennies then responded. When "Beth" explained how she had "intended to rake more leaves, but several other things came up that day," "Sue" said, "That's what always happens with you. You promise something, you don't do what you said—or you do half of it—and you always have these elaborate excuses. The bottom line is, you don't keep your word.

"I'd rather you tell me, 'I won't help you rake leaves.' Even better, I wish you would not always put those 'other' things first. I wish your priority would be to keep your word with me."

After a month, this family had noticeably fewer arguments. Their communications had definitely changed for the better. The two girls readily acknowledged they were not so emotionally "barricaded," or angry. Instead of always anticipating an excuse, and, therefore, being angry before the conversations with one another even started, they both said they could now listen and participate in conversations more openly.

"Everything is definitely much smoother and more loving," the parents said. "Even the baby is fretting and crying a lot less."

Write, Paint, Construct... Whatever Works!

Although this exercise is recommended for the entire family, sometimes it helps to offer it first for the children who are having difficulty with anger. Then invite the others to join in. Depending on your own family dynamics, one parent participating with one child may be best; or, both parents may participate with one child. You may start with one arrangement with parent and child, and then change. The process will let you know what is working and what is not.

The guidelines below anticipate one parent and one child. For everyone participating, however, the following understanding and agreements will help:

1. How you introduce the exercise is important. Suggest that its purpose is for the children to express—and for you to hear—some anger messages that will help you both.
2. How you prepare for the exercise is equally important. The nature of problematic anger is that it has accumulated from the past. For

some reason, these children did not successfully discharge the anger then. That anger is, therefore, stored with a memory that says, "It's not safe" or "It won't work for me to bring it up again." The problem, of course, is that the children have no control over the powerful patterns developed as a result of that suppressed anger. The memory inside says, "Hold it in." But the outward experience is, "I can't hold it in, and it's coming out in all kinds of ways I don't like."

It is important, therefore, for you to create a safe and non-judgmental, non-punitive emotional space inside yourself to absorb whatever you are going to hear. This means avoiding guilt or shame, or needing to explain or defend. These children need to identify this anger and report it now, so it does not continue to produce automatic, unproductive patterns. More than anything, they need to be *heard without consequences*. If you can empathize with the feelings underneath their anger (as the information on sadness and rage in *Conditions of Emotional Dysfunction* and *Transforming Anger Into Love*™ suggests), that will help you focus now on their needs, and not your own.

3. If your children are old enough to write—even single words or phrases—writing will help. Or, if because of age or choice, they would rather draw or paint, or build or create a project that helps identify and release the anger, any such expressive exercises will work. The more creative the better!

4. Reassure them that you want to help find the messages underneath the anger, and that the two of you will then discuss those messages. Also, reassure them of your commitment to do whatever you can to honor whatever those messages say. Remember: anger is a message about needs. (The Needs Exercise in *Lifestyles of the Stressed and Strained* will also help.) Humanity's principal need is for love. There are many ways to experience love, and somewhere inside these children is an unmet need for some kind of experience of love. That need was not met in the past, and its "demand" is still there.

Perhaps the need will not be met now. In instances of divorce, for example, the need can be related to feeling abandoned. "I need to not feel abandoned by my father," a child is likely to say when the anger and the need have been identified. In a way, you cannot do anything about the fact that you did divorce. The children cannot be with their birth father (or mother) every day. But through this exercise, you may help them release the sadness or fear or rage still embedded from that separation/abandonment trauma.

When that occurs, your love that is present and available can fill that space. With that new experience of love, the automatic patterns that regularly screamed, "I need to feel more love," can subside. The children now can feel more love pouring in.

5. Let your children know there is no time limit for this exercise. They can write or paint or create as long as the energy connected to their anger (or other suppressed emotions) is flowing forth. (The time frame does need to be set with some boundaries, of course. They do have to go to school and sleep and eat.) Also, emphasize that you want to provide whatever they say they need in order to "express." Many colored pens, perhaps. Different colors of paper. Even a large piece of paper, like butcher paper from the grocery store, where they want to depict a story. Stories can be very creative, and safe. Privacy may also be important, so help them create a safe space for their writing or pictures to be stored until they choose to share their project with you.

6. As the exercise unfolds, the children may come up with their own insights and answers. They may realize on their own, what they need to do or say or experience, that will help heal the anger (and perhaps other feelings) underneath. Encourage them to share with you what feelings or needs may be coming up. Let them know you want to be a part of helping them, but don't require this from them. In Indigo Children especially, their creativity and inner healing properties are astounding. Sometimes they simply need us to get out of the way.

7. Through the writing and reflecting and expressing, in the end, it is what they feel, and what they say, and what they need, that matters. As Melanie Melvin, Ph.D., emphasizes in the interview in Chapter Ten, Indigo Children need respect. They need to be

heard. They need their insights and feelings to matter. They surely need those experiences as they begin to open up and allow this exercise to work. Their anger may say to us that they did not feel they were listened to, or valued, or respected sufficiently in the past. With most children, it is never too late to listen, or to apologize, or to make new commitments that will help transform their anger into love.

Whatever we did as parents may not have been perfect or ideal, but it was always the best we could do at the time. As we have learned and matured since, our capacities also have matured. This is one of the reasons this exercise can work so well. It reaches into the spaces created in our children when we may not have been adequate, and this exercise allows us to fill those spaces from the capacities we have now. The children must be ready and willing to participate, of course. But bless their hearts—they so want to heal their anger. And they will give us *so* many chances, if we can simply hear their conditions and their needs.

In this book, and this exercise, we focus on the anger because in the end, we all want to feel more love.

Chapter Thirteen

Lifestyles of
the Stressed and Strained

An Exercise for Identifying Needs

Part I: For the Elders

This four-part exercise is designed to be helpful and insightful for both adults and children. Part I will help you better understand your needs, and better navigate your life in a manner that meets those needs. In turn, you will have a greater capacity to meet your children's needs as well as to assist them in attracting what they need. This information will benefit you whether you are a parent, a teacher, a counselor, or a friend of an Indigo Child.

The purpose of Part I is to help you identify which needs your current lifestyle and life choices are meeting and which needs they are not meeting. As you consider the topics in this exercise, you will view the activities and challenges in your life and see patterns, excesses, deficits, and needs.

Many topics in this book are in some manner connected to needs because anger is our emotional response when our needs are not met, while love is our emotional response when our needs *are* met. Since love is the emotion that manages anger, the more your lifestyle and life choices meet your needs, the more love you experience. The more love you experience, the more loving your responses can be for your children, your family, your friends, co-workers, community, etc.

This exercise is also about your relationship with self-love. The more love you experience, the more loving your responses can be in *your own* behalf. Be sure to consider your self and your relationship with self-love as you inventory your needs. Perhaps you are concerned that you are not spending enough quality time with those you love. Remember that it's important to ask if you're spending enough quality time with your self, as well. Adding to the quality and quantity of love inside can help you accept that your choices are the best ones you can make. Additional self-love might help you realize the toll those choices are taking, and you might rearrange your priorities.

As you complete Part I, notice your thoughts when the various topics are introduced. Especially pay attention to the first thought you have around a new topic. It might be about a person, a situation, or a memory. Maybe your first response might be a feeling. In the section on Love and Needs, you will read that thoughts are often clues about needs. With that in mind, realize that this Part I exercise can be a valuable tool in both identifying needs and in identifying which aspects of your life may be associated with those needs.

An example of noticing your response could be that when you see the topic "Time Alone," you roll your eyes. The reaction probably means you don't have a lot of time alone. What flashed through your mind when you first read that topic? Job? No childcare? Others' needs? It's likely that whatever or whomever you first thought about is a key to learning what to adjust in your life to ensure your need for time alone is met.

"But what if my needs are selfish?" you may wonder. And admittedly, finding balance among all the responsibilities and routines of daily-life these days can be very, very difficult—especially when the choices are between one's self and one's kids.

The truth is that self-love is not self-ish. Dedicating *some* time and energy to your self is being accountable and responsible. Doing so is also a good model for your children. It's important for them to experience an adult who values balance and who sets boundaries. Children need to learn about balance and boundaries for their own benefit and whatever you model is what they learn.

Another reason for making choices that meet *your* needs is that children do not want to feel that because of them, you have to sacrifice and do without. Children want time, energy, money, and other valuables to be shared. In addition, if they experience elders consistently making choices solely on their behalf, they may learn to expect the remainder of the world to do the same. This type of conditioning can make it difficult for children to share or to wait their turn.

Children are more of the focus in Parts II, III, and IV. If you have more than one child, do the exercise for each one. For now, however, allow this to be your time to focus on your needs.

A. My Needs in Relation to My Self

Rank on a scale of 1=low to 10=high.

For example, the first entry is "Honesty." An 8 in Column One would indicate that you have a strong need for honesty in your life. An 8 in Column Two would indicate that the need is met to a high degree. On the other hand, a 4 in Column Two would indicate that your need for honesty in your life is not being met to a high degree.

Column One		Column Two
How Strong This Need Is		**Degree To Which This Need Is Met**
_____	Honesty	_____
_____	Open Communication	_____
_____	Spirituality/Religion	_____
_____	Emotional Availability	_____
_____	Health Consciousness	_____
_____	Time Alone	_____
_____	Financial Security	_____
_____	Special Time With Others	_____
_____	Environmental Consciousness	_____
_____	Civic/Community/Volunteer Work	_____
_____	Travel	_____
_____	Fine Arts	_____
_____	Sports	_____
_____	Sense of Humor	_____
_____	Feeling Attractive	_____

How Strong This Need Is		Degree To Which This Need Is Met
_____	Time Management	_____
_____	Flexibility	_____
_____	TV/Videos/Movies	_____
_____	Patience	_____
_____	Continuing Education/Personal Growth	_____
_____	Music	_____
_____	Cooking/Eating Out	_____
_____	Keeping My Word	_____
_____	Reading	_____
_____	Exercise/Fitness	_____
_____	Order/Cleanliness	_____
_____	Sharing Responsibilities	_____
_____	Meditating	_____
_____	Touching/Being Touched	_____
_____	Shared Values	_____

Other: _____

On a separate sheet of paper, write your responses to the following:

B. What needs am I neglecting?

C. What patterns perpetuate that neglect?

D. What can I do to change the patterns?

E. What changes can I make so that my needs are met?

Part II: My Needs in Relation to My Child

On a separate sheet of paper, write your responses to the following for each child:

A. What are my needs in relation to my child?

B. In what ways are those needs being met?

C. In what ways are those needs not being met?

D. What changes can I make regarding my needs in relation to my child?

Part III: My Child's Needs As I Perceive Them

On a separate sheet of paper, write your response to the following for each child:

A. What are my child's needs as I perceive them?

B. In what ways are those needs being met?

C. In what ways are those needs not being met?

D. What changes can I make regarding my child's needs as I perceive them?

Part IV: My Child's Needs as Written or Expressed to Me

A. Ask your child to share this information in writing or in conversation. You may want the exercise to include individual needs, needs in the family, needs in school, needs related to friends, etc.

B. What are your child's needs as you now understand them?

C. In what ways are those needs being met?

D. In what ways are those needs not being met?

E. What changes can you make regarding your child's needs as you understand them?

Summary

On a separate sheet of paper, write your response to the following:

A. What I have learned from this exercise.

B. Changes I will make as a result of this exercise.

C. What do I know to be the patterns that often sabotage my efforts to change?

D. What can I do to ensure those patterns do not sabotage my efforts this time?

Notes

Chapter Fourteen

Anger, Rage
and the Possibilities for Change

1. Love is the creative emotion. It creates life itself. In an ideal
   world we would all experience sufficient love to create a meaningful, fulfilling, prosperous life. With that, anger would not be
   necessary. When love has not created the conditions we need,
   anger is the emotional tool that helps us interact with those conditions and ideally make them better. In such situations, anger is
   given the opportunity to improve the situation... which contrasts
   drastically with the properties of rage.

   Rage does not improve anything. It destroys everything on its
   path. Rage indicates the degree to which we feel powerless to create the conditions we need. Rage indicates the degree to which
   we desperately need to experience love. Rage indicates how desperately inadequate we feel in terms of connecting with the love
   we need.

2. Anger is an automatic emotional response that arises when our
   needs are not met. Unlike rage, anger is not an unloving, unfair,
   uncontrolled emotion. But it becomes so when too many needs
   are unmet for too long. If our own anger is out of control, we have
   lost touch with our needs. It means that we are continuing to

make choices that disregard our basic needs. The longer we continue this pattern, the greater will be the buildup of anger.

To change this destructive pattern, we must make some of our unmet needs a greater priority. The more choices we make that meet our needs, the greater our capacity to manage our anger. If we have lost touch with our needs, the following list will help us recognize which aspects of our life we have been neglecting.

- Having time alone
- Music
- Art
- Writing
- Meditating
- Spending time with friends
- Sleeping late
- Eating out
- Taking a trip
- Reading
- Exercising
- Enjoying intimacy
- Being out of doors
- Having flowers in your home
- Renewing spiritual practices
- Making better food choices '
- Having peace and quiet
- Managing your time to your advantage
- Exiting unfulfilling or abusive situations
- Making better financial decisions
- Keeping your house in order
- Spending quality time with your children
- Repairing your car
- Going to movies or to the theater
- Visiting relatives

3. Love is an automatic emotional response when our needs are met. Managing anger is an emotional responsibility, and the emotion that helps us manage it is love. If our anger is out of control, we are losing self-respect and feeling less self-love. We're saying

things we don't mean; doing things we regret; and reacting in ways that neither we nor anyone else can trust.

If this applies to you, you can reverse this by starting with one aspect of yourself you really want to change. During the times when you are *not* angry, focus on this aspect of yourself. Review in your mind how your anger usually escalates and brings out this part of you. Identify the moment when the usual anger-based, automatic patterns engage.

Throughout the day, rehearse in your mind how you can respond differently when those times occur. When that familiar triggering moment arises next time, remember your new commitment to yourself and act on it. Find the power you have been gathering inside and use it at that moment to make a different choice. If you often engage in these patterns with someone in particular—like your children—ask them to help you change at those times. Create a couple of sentences they can say that will remind you of your commitment to change. You will feel so much better when you access the power to change these patterns. With this important start, you will be able to change more and more patterns.

4. The purpose of anger is to produce change. The disruptive properties of anger are designed to interact in a situation that does not meet our needs, and rearrange the situation so that it does meet our needs. If the intensity of our anger is not sufficient to create the changes we need outside of ourselves, then our anger is telling us we either need to change situations, or, make some changes inside ourselves.

5. Anger is a normal, even appropriate response, to certain everyday life events. Rage, on the other hand, is an accumulation of unexpressed anger—generally years of unexpressed anger. Although anger is a more intense emotion than love, love is more enduring. Because of this, anger does not displace love; but rage does. In an angry exchange, a person can be very angry but still be in touch with love. When a person is angry but *not* in touch with love, that is either a developmental stage of rage, or the actual condition of rage.

6. If you or someone you know is engaged in the automatic, destructive reactions of rage, the emotion underneath is sadness. Sadness is our response to the loss of love. Every time that automatic pattern of rage engages, it compounds the loss of love, especially self-love. If the sadness can be released on its own, it will help diminish the power of the rage. Instead of being concerned about getting in touch with the sadness or understanding it, focus on allowing yourself to feel it. The sadness is underneath all the time. The only reason you do *not* feel it is that your emotional defense mechanisms keep it suppressed.

Those mechanisms were probably developed early in life when you did not experience adequate love. At that time, when you were a small child, the sadness may have felt overwhelming—even unbearable. In response, a healthy, protective part of you sealed off that sadness. Now, however, the sadness represents, and consumes, part of your emotional power. Working to keep it suppressed consumes so much energy, however, that you may not feel the power. You may even feel power*less* in connection with the sadness. The healing process for sadness allows it to come up and be released. At that point, you will be free from needing the intensity of rage as an emotional protection mechanism.

If you allow the sadness to be released when it does comes up—at the grocery store, driving on the freeway, in the shower—trust the timing and don't send it back down. The fact that strangers you will never see again may see you cry must be less important than your own emotional transformation and healing.

7. Anger is a proportional emotion. As such, it can be trusted. Unlike rage, anger wells up inside us in proportion to the incident that causes it. A minor incident will evoke a raised tone of voice. A deliberate abuse will activate a much more powerful response.

If you find yourself expressing more anger than the situation calls for, you are drawing from the reservoir of unexpressed anger—the reservoir that accumulates and turns into rage. When this happens, stop the exchange the moment you recognize your response is out of balance. Acknowledge at that moment that you are behaving in a manner that is unacceptable. Apologize if you indeed feel regret and allow a different part of yourself to come forward.

It is understandable if you can't imagine that you have other options at times like that. The automatic patterns of rage have undoubtedly prevailed at those times in the past. You can, however, develop new options to those patterns by using your courage and power to at least stop the expression of the rage. That's how you create the space needed to discover and implement a new option.

Because rage is automatic and uncontrolled, sometimes you may have to utter some "filler" words, just to allow the energy underneath the rage to come forth without being damaging. For example, when you realize you are automatically engaged (again), you might say, "I know what I usually say and do at this time, and I want to do something different now. I don't know what else to do, but at least I am letting you know I *want* to do and say something different this time. If you can help me right now, by saying something that will help calm and redirect this situation, then please do so. I am trying to avoid the destructive things I usually say and do... and I could use your help."

When you access the power inside yourself to intercept and reverse an unproductive exchange, you regain your sense of self-respect and self-love. After a few successful efforts at intercepting the patterns of uncontrolled anger, you will have diminished the power of those patterns. In that manner, you will be able to replace them with more trustworthy, loving options.

8. The hidden message behind anger is, "I need to feel more love." When you are angry, instead of blasting the outside world and circumstances, examine what your anger indicates about your relationship to love. Your anger is an effort to change something outside yourself. It may also be an indication of something needing to change inside. If so, some way you are behaving is *really* bothering you. You recognize that it is counterproductive, and that so long as you continue being that way, the results will not be positive. Instead of maturely commencing the change you need to

make inside yourself, perhaps you rail at the outside world wanting it to change instead. When the love you need to feel is in relation to yourself, your outward anger will not only make matters worse. It will also waste the productive possibilities of anger.

9. Whereas love is the enduring emotion, anger is designed to be a non-enduring emotion. Its properties are purposefully uncomfortable so that we don't hold onto it and allow it to accumulate into rage. Sometimes we deny or hide our anger because we think that doing so will make us more appealing or attract more love to us. The absolute opposite is true, however. Developing an internal inferno inside ensures we will be attract**ed** to and attract**ive** to people who have similar reservoirs of rage. Emotionally healthy people will sense our rage and will want to avoid getting emotionally singed by avoiding *us*. They may not recognize that it is our hidden rage that keeps them at a distance. They will simply not return phone calls, or they will be unavailable for lunch every time we inquire.

10. Unexpressed anger keeps us tied to the past. So long as it is stored up inside us, it keeps us remembering all the arguments; all the incidents; all the abuse; all the blame; all the times we felt criticized, ignored, lied to, and shamed. All the past times when we were not understood, not valued, not nurtured, not supported, not given a chance, not treated fairly, and especially, not loved. So long as those memories are accessible, they can ruin a perfectly nice day by invading our consciousness and causing us to relive those conditions as though they were happening again. Now. Forever, in fact, unless we halt those memories as they come up and direct our attention toward being productive in our life at present. Indulging the memories gives them power. Overriding them gives us hope.

11. Anger is to be expressed at the time and to the degree it is felt. It is then released, and the enduring emotion of love returns. If we manipulate the anger by denying or suppressing it, then our anger becomes manipulative. It loses its integrity. It becomes untrustworthy and unloving. To reclaim our emotional integrity requires honesty about our anger, saying at the moment the anger comes

up: "I'm feeling angry; this is what I'm angry about; and this is the change I need."

Expressing the anger and releasing it enables it to serve its purpose—to challenge a situation to rearrange so it can meet our needs. Expressing the anger ensures it cannot accumulate and become the uncontrolled, uncontrollable, destructive condition of rage.

Summary

If we have sufficient love in our life, we use love to create what we need. If we have sufficient love in our life, we use love to transform anger into patience, understanding, compassion, renegotiation and forgiveness.

If we increasingly experience anger, it is a message about love. To increase our experience of love, the message is about needs.

Managing anger is an emotional responsibility, and the emotion that manages anger is love. To feel more love in our life we must do things that are good for us; do things we enjoy; do things that meet our needs; and be the type of person we can respect and love.

Notes

Anger and the Indigo Child

Chapter Fifteen

Indigo Essence

Indigo Essence

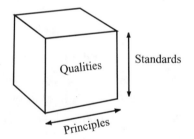

The primary rule is to have fewer rules, and more
guidelines and principles of behavior.

~ Melanie Melvin, Ph.D.[1]

While each of us has our own purpose and potential, Indigo Children are often attuned to theirs at a very early age. In addition, their awareness of their purpose and potential may manifest in unique and specific ways. For example, it is not uncommon for toddler Indigo Children to talk knowingly about what they are to "do" as a career or contribution to humanity. Young Indigo Children also often talk about how they are to "Be." One of the Indigo indicators is that they possess a deep desire to help the world in a big way. While some Indigo Children may not know the form of their contribution to humanity—inventor, humanitarian, entrepreneur, or artist—Indigo Children know they have significant gifts, and that those gifts have a purpose.

As a result, Indigo Children identify with their gifts and purpose in a manner that parents have described as protective, intense, unwavering, and even unnerving.

This knowing can be part of the challenge that Indigo Children bring to families and classrooms. It is, however, part of the essence of Indigo Children. Understanding the three principal components of that essence will enable us all to help these children manifest their extraordinary purpose and potential.

PRINCIPLES: How They Know

> *It is necessary for the salvation of man,*
> *That certain truths which exceed human reason,*
> *Should be made known to him by divine revelation.*
>
> ~ St. Thomas Aquinas

The previous three books on Indigo Children speak comprehensively to these children's spirituality. While that is not the focus of this writing, their spirituality is certainly one of the foremost aspects of Indigo Children. They do "know." They know who they are, what they feel, what they need, and what they are to "do" with their lives. That knowing is sometimes characterized as part of their divine essence. As Kitty, the grandmother quoted in Chapter Two, says of holding her grandson for the first time, "I knew he was an ancient soul."

In order to manifest their knowing-ness, Indigo Children rely on principles: universal, spiritual, philosophical, psychological, etc. Because principles are the basis for *how* these children know, and *what* they know, principles are also the foundation for how Indigo Children learn to express and implement their knowing-ness, and their Being. Stewarding and facilitating that exchange of their knowing and their Being is one of the most important roles for us, the elders.

Principles are the axis of exchange between what Indigo Children know and how they know, and what they are to learn and how they are to learn. In an ideal "educational" setting, Indigo Children would tell us, the elders, what they need to know. Then we, as their "educators," would be responsible for gathering the information they need and presenting it in a manner that meets their needs. They would ask the questions and we would provide the answers.

Indigo Children know what they need to know. They also know what they do not need to know. This is one of the reasons these children often have difficulty in mainstream educational systems. It is also why many of these children do better in a whole-brain, holistic, individualized learning environment. These settings and education models are more eclectic and co-created.

In the future, it will serve Indigo Children to create the model for their own individual learning styles and needs. In any learning environment, at home or at school, Indigo Children are best served by being asked for their input before being told what to learn or how to learn. The educators quoted in the previous Indigo books offer many insights into this aspect of Indigo Children's educational needs and processes.

STANDARDS: How They Do

Indigo Children have their own standards. These standards specifically complement their gifts and potential. Indigo Children hold steadfastly to their standards. As a result, sometimes these children are labeled as perfectionists. Sometimes they spend far longer than other children when completing a creative task or project. These aspects of Indigo Children are yet another reason they often have difficulty fitting into standardized classrooms and curriculum.

Indigo Children see details and intricacies that others, both elders and other children, do not see. They rejoice in the expression of those details and intricacies. They often ask for lots of colors—like, many colored markers, many colors of felt-tip pens, many pieces and colors of paper, and ribbons, and objects of many shapes and textures. For them, this is not indulgent. It is their creativity seeking expression. If our tendency is to rush them, or insist that they be satisfied with our standards rather than meeting their own, this can evoke their anger.

Indigo Children *love* their gifts and potential. They love executing a project in accordance with all the talents and excellence in their Being. To do so is indeed an element of their self-actualization. If we can learn to trust their standards, and help them find people and places in their lives to understand and complement those standards, we will facilitate these children's adjustment and expression immeasurably.

This is especially true in their employment possibilities. As these children mature and are expected to merge their gifts and talents into the workforce and economic mainstream, it will help them to apply the following guidelines for both preserving and expressing their exceptional qualities and gifts.

Guidelines for the Gifted

- Your gifts are specifically created to complement and fulfill your own unique purpose and potential.
- Your gifts, which are different from your abilities and talents, are reserved for your own exceptional contribution to the world.
- Your gifts are dedicated to your own purpose. They will not be unleashed to fit into or complement any other individual's or entity's purpose.
- You may apprentice in the world as you train for stewarding your gifts, and for fulfilling your own unique, valuable contribution. Those apprenticeships will not utilize your gifts. They will train you to manage and mature your gifts. In so doing, those apprenticeships may utilize and benefit from your abilities and talents. Then, in accordance with the timing and manifestation of your own purpose and potential, your gifts will be readied and incorporated.
- You will recognize your apprenticeships by the people rather than the job. In these situations, you are looking for the next teacher, mentor, or role model. When you find that person, that is how you recognize your next work environment or job opportunity.
- Those apprenticing environments may not recognize, or appreciate, or compensate you for your exceptional capabilities.
- Unless they do so—and only in proportion to how they do so— you are to find a way to do an excellent job in accordance with

the job description and compensation you are offered.

- To exceed those parameters, just because you have the ability to do so, is both a waste of your gifts, and also a disservice to environments that are not calibrated to integrate them.
- When you have attracted the resources—fiscal, human, and creative—to implement your purpose and potential, then you are to unleash your gifts and potential fully and magnificently.
- Until then, the challenge is to reduce your own standards to meet others' highest expectations and standards.

QUALITIES: How They Be

- Indigo Children recognize and rely on qualities within. Their qualities are the key to their essence. Qualities are also the essence they seek out in others.
- Indigo Children seek the presence of love and the integrity of truth.
- Indigo Children exalt in embodying the universal principle, "The greatest good for the greatest number."
- Indigo Children seek and value fairness, balance, equity, and honesty.
- Indigo Children seek justness and justice. They resist and resent an individual or environment that is enabling or inadequate, permissive or indulgent, exploitative or punitive.
- Indigo Children seek and respect emotional integrity. They know when others' anger is out of proportion. They know when apology or regret is called for. They detach and protect from individuals who lack emotional integrity.
- Indigo Children seek and respect emotional maturity. They resist and resent the limitations of elders who cannot honor these children's emotional intelligence, and steward these children's own emotional maturity. Indigo Children particularly resist and resent elders who punish and control because they lack the emotional adequacy to do otherwise.
- Indigo Children seek accountability, both within themselves and in others. They like to be taught to keep their word, and to be held to other high standards of individual accountability and

responsibility. They appreciate accountability modeled in their environments, even though they may employ considerable energy to see if they can get by with something lesser.

- Indigo Children are attuned to the order of the universe. They seek order in their own lives and Being. They may have their own sense of order, and they may rigorously protect the order they have established and need in their lives.

- Indigo Children seek harmony with their environment and with all life forms.

- Indigo Children seek balance in economic, financial, and money-related matters.

- Indigo Children have an innate set of values to complement their purpose and potential. They seek individuals and environments compatible with their values, and resist individuals and environments non-complementary to their values.

- Indigo Children have a sense of self-value and self-worth. They seek individuals and environments that confirm their value and worth, and resist individuals and environments incompatible with their self-value and self-worth.

- Indigo Children seek to make the world better, not the ego greater. Their sense of individual and collective ego is acute. They seek balance with the ego, the body, the mind, and the soul.

Chapter Sixteen

The Anger Work™

Anger Resolution™ Training and Certification

The Anger Resolution Axis™ Model

A. Background

This training and certification program and the information contained herein are based on the Anger Resolution Axis™ method of understanding and resolving anger and anger-related patterns. It is a model developed by the author, who founded the Anger Management Institute, and who began teaching this information while president of a stress management company in 1983.

B. Purpose of this Program

The purpose of the Anger Resolution Specialist™ Training and Certification Program is to create a new discipline—a para-profession—to complement existing education and credentialing for (1) individuals in the broad range of health and human services, as well as (2) individuals working in behalf of others' education and well-being in a variety of settings.

These categories include, for example, nurses and physicians, counselors and therapists, social workers, clergy, teachers and coaches, domestic violence staff, youth and adult detention personnel, foster care and adoption parents and personnel, home healthcare providers, attorneys and judges, human resources officers, employee assistance program administrators— together with parents and any other individuals who seek in-depth insight and comprehensive how-to skills for identifying and resolving the anger-based patterns that compromise love, happiness, health, and success.

C. Principal Components of the Anger Resolution Axis™ Model:

- Identifying and Reversing The Emotional Dysfunction Grids™
- Implementing The Emotion Modification™ Model
- Transforming The Conditions Matrix™
- Transforming The UnLove/Anger/Rage Axis™
- Transforming The UnLove/Fear/Sadness/Needs Axis™
- Implementing The Anger Resolution Axis™

D. Introduction of Terms

1. Identifying and Reversing The Emotional Dysfunction Grids™

The term *grids* is used as an image to represent the configuration of emotional energies compromised and interlocking as a result of suppression. *Suppression* refers to an automatic, non-conscious redirection of certain emotional energy which was not expressed at the time it was activated within, thereby resulting in a behavior (passive *or* active) which, at the moment of the emotional activation, lacked the full integration of the (suppressed) emotion. *Emotional dysfunction* is used to describe the outcome of the automatic patterns that result from emotions continually not being integrated with behavior.

This program teaches both how to identify the presence of emotional dysfunction as a result of the suppressed emotions, and how to reverse the configuration of emotional energies formed therefrom.

2. Implementing The Emotion Modification™ Model

While the term "behavior modification" is well-known in the mental health field, the Anger Resolution™ model creates a new emphasis on emotional healing: *Emotion Modification™*. The premise of this model is that without adequate and contemporaneous emotion modification, behavior modification lacks the properties and sustainability essential to

Anger Resolution™. Accordingly, the term Anger Resolution™ is used in this program to distinguish this approach from traditional approaches to anger management.

Specifically inherent in this program is the premise that anger, as a proportional, purposeful emotion, does not require management. More specifically, inherent in this program are the distinction between anger and rage, and a method for reversing rage by resolving the interlocking dysfunctional emotional patterns (grids) that suppressed emotions have formed, thereby producing an accumulation of unexpressed anger that has developed the properties of rage.

This program teaches *Emotion Modification*™ as a process to reverse and transform suppressed emotions so that love is accessible and integrated.

3. Transforming The Conditions Matrix™

The term *matrix* is used as an image to represent the configuration of emotional energies so compromised and entangled as a result of suppression—so non-dynamic, unintegrated and unavailable—that they no longer represent an emotional state: they have instead become a condition. The term *condition* is used to describe the product of automatically suppressed emotional energies that result in a behavior formed specifically to ensure the emotions remain non-dynamic, unintegrated and unavailable.

This program teaches how to identify and transform those conditions so that emotional power, maturity, and security can result.

4. Transforming The UnLove/Anger/Rage Axis™

The term *axis* refers to the continuum along which certain emotional patterns and conditions develop as a result of automatically suppressed emotions. The word *UnLove* is used to refer both to the experience of living one's life, either in whole or in part, without experiencing love, as well as living one's life (in whole or in part) in the presence of actions, behaviors and experiences that were particularly *un*-loving—such as abusive or exploitative.

In addressing this axis, this program teaches the distinction between anger and rage; the patterns and behaviors that develop from each of those; and the stations along the anger/rage axis wherein principles of transformation can be implemented to produce the experience of love.

5. Transforming The UnLove/Fear/Sadness/Needs Axis™

Since the outcomes of long-term emotional suppression are complex, more than one axis model is used in this program to describe the interrelated and progressive emotional patterns that develop as a result. In addressing this axis, this program teaches how to transform the specific subsidiary fear- and sadness-related emotional patterns that result from unmet needs for love.

6. Implementing The Anger Resolution Axis™

Although it is in Level Four of this training program that full competency to implement The Anger Resolution Axis™ is obtained, Levels One, Two and Three of this training program consistently include principles for that implementation—which is to help people experience more love.

Accordingly, Levels Two and Three of this program are experientially designed to ensure that each participant in the program is given the principles, insights, support and opportunity to identify and transform his/her own emotional patterns so that the power contained therein can be unleashed first for the individual's emotional development and competency—and then so that individual can model and teach others to do the same.

The Emotional Wellness Institute

Presents

The Anger Work™

A Training and Certification Program

Developed By

Dianne Lancaster
Boulder, Colorado
Emotional Wellness Institute

Anger Management Training and Certification

Program Description: Certificate Series

Each of the following three levels of training leads to a certificate for completing the stated curriculum. Certificates are for:

- Anger Management   (Level I)
- Anger Reduction™   (Level II)
- Anger Resolution™   (Level III)

Materials distinguishing between the curriculum, application and competency levels for each are available upon request. This is solely for review by persons interested in supporting this project.

Certificate Series -- Level I

Introduction to Anger Management Principles

Format: Two weekend workshops:
Saturday, 9 a.m. – 6 p.m. and Sunday, 9 a.m. – 4 p.m.

Emphasis: Personal Growth.

Audience: For anyone seeking greater understanding of anger, anger-based patterns, rage, and skills for managing unproductive emotions. Ideal for individuals, parents, partners, teachers, coaches, clergy, attorneys, guidance counselors, human resource and EAP personnel, probation officials, health practitioners, divorce recovery, childcare and home care providers, foster care and adoptive parents, business owners, managers, employees and persons in high-stress or burnout mode.

Dates: Spring

Participant Fees: $395 including materials

Description: Understanding the purpose of anger; healthy vs. unproductive ways to express it; the Hidden Symptoms of Anger™; transgenerational patterns that suppressed anger creates; automatic triggering mechanisms; and related patterns that compromise love, happiness, health, and success.

Participants will be taught how to recognize and address these anger-based patterns in personal life situations, relationships, family, schools, workplace, and community.

Certificate Series -- Level II

Integrated Anger Reduction™ Principles and Strategies

Format: Two weekend workshops:
Saturday, 9 a.m. – 6 p.m. and Sunday, 9 a.m. – 4 p.m.

Emphasis: Additional interactive skills for anger reduction, mediation, prevention and intervention.

Audience: Graduates of Level I.

Application: Adds additional interactive skills and competency to Level I curriculum, enabling graduates to apply Integrated Anger Reduction™ Principles and Strategies in behalf of clients, patients, students, employees, families, partners, individuals, customers, constituencies, and others in existing programs/protocols.

This expertise can be utilized in schools, businesses, faith-based organizations and institutions, employee assistance and human resource programs, abused children, child advocacy, foster care and adoption programs, women's shelters, crisis hotlines, addictions recovery programs, spousal abuse programs, divorce and estate mediation, residential treatment, nursing and group homes, home health care, hospice, vocational rehabilitation and training, detention centers, probation programs, adolescent counseling and treatment programs, and other similar environments.

Dates: Summer

Participant Fees: $495 including materials

Description: Recognizing and redirecting patterns locked into and creating **The Anger Grid™**, wherein underlying anger-based patterns produce dysfunctional outcomes such as emotional detachment, estrangement, alienation and abandonment; withdrawal, manipulation, defensiveness and control; denial, projection, shame and blame; guilt, anxiety, apathy, revenge; codependence, victim identity, abuse cycle participation, and chronic crises syndrome.

Also, addictions, depression, stress, food disorders, financial imbalance, compromised ethics and integrity, compromised self-worth and self-trust, self-respect and self-love, self-care, and life-management skills.

Participants will be taught how to integrate principles and strategies to reduce these types of anger-based patterns in personal life situations, relationships, family, schools, workplace, and community.

Certificate Series -- Level III

Applied Anger Resolution™ Strategies

Format: Two weekend workshops:
Saturday, 9 a.m. – 6 p.m. and Sunday, 9 a.m. – 4 p.m.

Emphasis: Principles, models and skills for reversing past, present and pending consequences of the uncontrolled, uncontrollable, destructive outcomes of rage.

Audience: Graduates of Levels I and II.

Application: Adds vital skills for persons in above Level I and II Application categories and environments, enabling them to assist others in transforming self-destructive patterns and conditions, whether manifested or accumulating, and replace those patterns with sustainable emotional competency, adequacy and equilibrium. Applies to any situation or environment wherein underlying anger-related issues compromise safety, security, personal or family well-being, productivity, profits, performance, quality assurance, morale, education, personal growth, emotional and physical boundaries, emotional and physical health, spiritual well-being.

Dates: Fall

Participant Fees: $495 including materials

Description: Applies the Emotion Modification™ Model to recognize, address and redirect patterns functioning along **The Anger/ Rage Axis™**.

Participants will be taught how to identify and neutralize destructive, uncontrolled aspects and conditions of emotional dysfunction—including the internalized and externalized, self- and other-directed, manifestations of rage—by applying Anger Resolution™ Strategies that reverse the presence and outcomes of rage in personal life situations, relationships, family, schools, and workplace.

Applicable in established protocols such as those already listed in Levels I and II; plus court-mandated programs, groups and classes.

These three Certificate Series levels are prerequisites for Level IV Certification.

Total Fees for Levels I, II and III:	$1,385	per person
(Plus Level IV described below)	<u>1,685</u>	per person
Total: Levels I – IV	$3,070	per person

Program Description -- Level IV

Intermediate Anger Management Certification™

Format: Five-day or 3-weekend individualized intensive study and training leading to Intermediate Anger Management Certification™

Emphasis: Personal and professional development and competency for teaching, group facilitation, staff development, and individual coaching.

Audience: Graduates of Levels I, II and III.

Application: Based on participant's background, participant's Level I, II and III acquired competency, and participant's emphasis of study within this program's selection of topics, graduates of this certification program will qualify for para-professional positions in existing programs/protocols; as independent contractors/ consultants; teachers of selected classes, workshops and seminars; group facilitators; corporate and organizational staff development; and as an individual Emotional Wellness Coach™. This certification is also prerequisite to training and staff positions within the Emotional Wellness Institute's ongoing Anger Management Training and Certification Program.

Dates: To Be Announced

Participant Fees: $1,685 including materials

Description: This training is designed to offer specialized expertise applicable to individuals, relationships, parents, families, groups, schools, workplace, and community.

While the basic curriculum for Level IV is consistent for all certification groups, each group does select certain "electives" to focus on, based on individual interests and desire for expanded expertise. Topics from which those electives are selected include the following spectrum of human needs, conditions, unresolved issues, and dysfunctions:

- Transforming Anger Into Love™
- Self-Love
- The Anger-to-Rage Developmental Process™
- Resolving Family of Origin Issues
- Grief, Anger and Unresolved Emotional Patterns Related to Loss of Loved One
- Identifying and Reducing Anger in the Workplace
- Working Within the System: Probation, Court-Mandated Anger Management, etc.
- Reversing the Continual Crisis Syndrome
- 12 Steps to Anger Management
- The Warning Signs
- Eating Disorders
- Anger as a Spiritual Teacher™ / The Spiritual Dimensions of Anger™
- Managing the Angry Child™
- Divorce Recovery
- Mending the Family that Money Has Torn Apart
- Seduction, Exploitation and Abandonment: Why Relationships Fail™
- For the Children's Sake™: Transforming the Childhood Patterns Perpetuated by Parents
- Disciplining with Love™
- When You're Angry With Your Illness and Your Anger Makes You Ill™

It is the goal of this intensive training certification to facilitate, model, teach, and transfer to participants the principles and dynamics for emotional wellness so that participants can use that emotional competency and adequacy to accomplish the purpose and potential of this training certification: to help people experience more love by transforming the anger-based patterns that compromise their relationship with love.

Glossary of Terms

Anger Bypass™ depicts the tendency to disregard anger, often because of the (erroneous) fear that expressing it will compromise the availability of love.

The Anger Grid™ depicts the underlying configuration of anger-based patterns that are locked into fixed emotional responses. These grid-like configurations form in an individual whose anger is dysfunctional. These grids can also be activated when two or more individuals with dysfunctional patterns engage in repeated, unproductive exchanges. These exchanges then produce **Anger GridLock**™. The consequences of enacting these grids rather than transforming the emotionally dysfunctional patterns comprising them can produce dysfunctional outcomes such as emotional detachment, estrangement, alienation, and abandonment; withdrawal, manipulation, defensiveness, and control; denial, projection, shame, and blame; guilt, anxiety, apathy, revenge; codependence, victim identity, abuse cycle participation, and chronic crises syndrome.

The Anger/Love Axis™ depicts a continuum along which the individual's relationship with anger either functions in a manner that challenges love to expand; or the anger accumulates in a manner that compromises that individual's relationship with love. In The Anger Work™ and the Principles for Transforming Anger Into Love™, any principles applied to an individual's anger-based patterns are complemented by principles for increasing the presence of love.

Anger/Rage Axis™ depicts a continuum along which the individual's relationship with anger is steadily suppressed to the degree that it is loses proportionality, becomes uncontrollable, and builds up to the extent it destroys the individuals' connection to love, including self-love. At that end stage, the energy along the continuum is functioning in the rage range rather than the anger range.

The Anger Resolution Axis™ depicts a continuum along which the individual's relationship with anger is plotted according to the presence of love, anger, fear, and sadness, and the dysfunctional conditions created by sustained suppression of one or more of those emotions. Accordingly, resolving the anger-based patterns and conditions requires a matching relationship with love.

The Anger Work™ is the name given to the Anger Management, Anger Reduction, and Anger Resolution™ Training and Certification created to credential individuals at the para-professional level of applied techniques and principles for Transforming Anger Into Love™. The principal components of this model include:
- Identifying and Reversing The Emotional Dysfunction Grids™
- Implementing The Emotion Modification™ Model
- Transforming The Conditions Matrix™
- Transforming The UnLove/Rage Axis™
- Transforming The UnLove/Sadness Axis™
- Transforming the Needs/Capacities Axis™
- Implementing The Anger Resolution Axis™

Axis depicts the continuum along which emotions interact, and also the continuum along which suppressed emotional patterns and conditions develop. In the Transforming Anger Into Love™ model, an axis describes emotions, or conditions, or a combination, each one of which is vying for the energy located along that axis.

Dysfunctional depicts the behavioral and emotional results of automatic patterns that render suppressed emotions unavailable, unintegrated with behavior and needs, and therefore compromising the individual's relationship with love.

Conditions depict a non-dynamic, unproductive, dysfunctional state that develops as the result of significant, usually long-term buildup of suppressed emotions. Conditions render emotional energy unavailable, thereby diluting the individual's emotional power and security, and also the individual's emotional integrity and maturity. Because conditions originate due to suppressed anger, they compromise the individual's relationship with love.

Emotional Dysfunction depicts the outcome of cumulative anger-based patterns resulting from suppressed emotions, therefore not being integrated with behavior, and continually compromising the individual's relationship with love.

Emotional GridLock™ depicts the energy patterns of suppressed emotions intersecting in a fixed and entangled manner to the degree they produce automatic, unproductive, anger-based patterns of emotional dysfunction.

Emotion Modification™ depicts the value, as well as the capacity, for ensuring that any model or system seeking to modify behavior, as a manifestation of emotional dysfunction, successfully modifies the emotional patterns accompanying that behavior, as well. Specifically in connection with anger, Emotion Modification™ ensures that efforts to modify behavior also increase the individual's relationship with love, because it is the emotion that manages anger.

Engagable Rage™ depicts the capacity and inevitability of rage—the uncontrolled, uncontrollable buildup of anger—to engage, even though it has been successfully denied or suppressed for a period of time. This threat to emotional integrity and well-being exists unless direct, successful principles of Rage Reversal™ have been implemented with Emotion Modification ™ strategies and implementation.

The Gifted/Damaged Axis™ depicts the continuum along which an individual's exceptional gifts and potential are plotted in tandem with almost equivalent self- and other-destructive potential and inclination.

Grids™ depict an image of intersecting energy fields that represent the configuration of emotional energies compromised and entangled as a result of suppression.

Grid(un)Lock™ depicts strategies for identifying and reversing patterns created by suppressed anger that engage (lock) two or more individuals in automatic, unproductive behaviors, and replacing the energies of those patterns with self-loving, integrated behaviors and emotional availability for all individuals locked into the patterns.

Hidden Symptoms of Anger™ are depicted as the energy of suppressed anger that is stored in the body and makes its subtle presence known by "body language" and other interpretive indicators that signal the presence of that anger.

The Love/Needs Axis™ depicts the continuum along which needs are identified and actions to meet those needs are successful, thereby producing love—humanity's emotional response when needs are met. This axis is used specifically to identify the inclination for an individual to represent the capacity to offer love, when the individual is actually more driven by the need for love.

The Needs/Capacities Axis™ depicts the continuum along which an individual has the capacity, as opposed to the need, to fulfill certain commitments, or to meet certain needs, in connection with others. This axis is used specifically to identify the inclination of individuals to make commitments based on their needs, rather than their capacities, which inclination is often the product a deep-seated unproductive pattern that regularly results in unfulfilled commitments, unmet needs, and anger.

Rage depicts the condition that results when an individual has suppressed both anger and fear to such a degree that those emotional energies fuse together and produce a condition that is uncontrolled, uncontrollable, lacks emotional conscience, and is detached from emotional intervention.

Rage Reversal™ depicts a strategy for reversing anger-based patterns that have evolved into rage, by enabling the individual to reclaim a connection with self-love, and then utilize the destructive properties of rage to eliminate the unproductive patterns compromising the individual's relationship with love.

Rage/Sadness Axis™ depicts the continuum along which an individual accumulates sadness in connection with UnLove as a result of the buildup of rage that destroys that individual's connection with love.

Suppression is depicted in contrast to the expression of an emotion. When an emotion is activated but not expressed, it is suppressed. Suppression is an automatic, non-conscious redirection of emotional energy that results in behavior (passive or active) that lacks the full integration, acknowledgment, integrity, and accountability of the suppressed emotion.

UnLove™ depicts the experience of a child who may be in the presence of love, but does not necessarily experience that love; therefore, the child experiences UnLove™.

Notes

Quoted Material

1 Quoted from the book: *The Indigo Children.*
2 Quoted from the book: *The Care and Feeding of Indigo Children.*
3 Quoted from the video: *Super Brain Kids: Are They Born... or Made?*
4 Quoted from the book: *the Ritalin Fact Book.*
5 Quoted from the book: *Talking Back to Ritalin.*
6 Quoted from the compact disk: *Living Room Suite.*

Notes

Resources

Books:

Carlson, Nancy. *Snowden*. New York: Penguin Group, 1997.

Carroll, Lee, & Tober, Jan. *The Indigo Children*. California: Hay House, 1999.

Carroll, Lee, & Tober, Jan. *An Indigo Celebration*. California: Hay House, 2001.

Firmage, George. (Ed.) *E. E. Cummings: A Miscellany Revised*. New York: October House, 1955.

Hadady, Letha. *Asian Health Secrets*. New York: Crown Publishers, 1996.

Hay, Louise. *Heal Your Body*. California: Hay House, 1982.

Keleman, Stanley. *Emotional Anatomy*. California: Center Press, 1985.

Kushi, Michio, *Oriental Diagnosis: What Your Face Reveals*. London: Sunwheel Publications, 1978.

Muramoto, Naboru. *Healing Ourselves*. New York: Avon Books, 1973.

Page, Linda. *Healthy Healing*. California: Healthy Healing Publications, 1997.

Virtue, Doreen. *The Care and Feeding of Indigo Children*.
California: Hay House, 2001.

Video Tape:

Super Brain Kids: Are They Born... or Made? Grizzly Adams
Productions, Inc. Baker, OR, 2001.

Compact Disk:

Chapin, Harry. *Living Room Suite*. Elektra Entertainment 9 60628-
2. Chapin Music, 1978.

Professional Organizations:

American Montessori Society (AMS)
150 Fifth Avenue New York, NY 10011
212-924-3209

Association of Waldorf Schools of North America
3911 Bannister Rd. Fair Oaks, CA. 95628
916-961-0927
www.ch.steiner.school.nz/waldir.html

The National Center for Homeopathy
Toll free at (877) 624-0613 or at
www.homeopathic.org

To obtain the name of a certified homeopath:
The North American Society of Homeopaths
(206) 720-7000 www.homeopathy.org or
nashinfo@aol.com

The National Foundation for Gifted and Creative Children
395 Diamond Hill Road Warwick, RI. 02886
(401) 738-0937

Professionals

Barbra Gilman has 20 years' experience as a therapist and is a Certified Parent Educator with the International Network for Children and Families. CEO of Success Strategies for Life, Barbra is author of *The Unofficial Guide to Living Successfully on Planet Earth*. She can be reached at (888) 826-8930.

Debra Hegerle owns her own company, *Dragonfly Productions*, a bookkeeping and psychic consultancy business. She is an Indigo parent and a teacher's aide, and she volunteers for Compassion in Action in San Francisco and San Jose. She can be reached at Dragonfly Productions, P.O. Box 2674, Martinez, CA 94553

Abraham Maslow, 1908-1970, received his Ph.D. in 1934 in psychology from the University of Wisconsin. He published his first conceptual paper on the Hierarchy of Needs in 1943, and by the late 1960s he had become the leader of the humanistic school of psychology. At the top of Maslow's Hierarchy of Needs are the self-actualizing needs: to fulfill one's self, and to become all that one is capable of becoming.

Kathy A. McCloskey, Ph.D., Psy.D., is a licensed social worker and clinical psychologist who has worked with African-Americans, Appalachians, children, gays, transgendered, teens, battered women and their perpetrators, and the severely mentally ill. Contact her at: Ellis Human Development Institute, 9 N. Edwin C. Moses Blvd., Dayton, OH 45407

Judith Spitler McKee, Ed.D., is a developmental psychologist, growth counselor, and professor emerita of educational psychology and early childhood education at Eastern Michigan University. She is author of 12 textbooks on children's learning, development, play and creativity. Contact her by Fax at (248) 698-3961.

Melanie Melvin, Ph.D., DHM, RSHom, is a licensed psychologist and homeopath. She combines homeopathy and psychology for her clientele of both adults and children. Her interview is contained in Chapter Ten of this book. Contact her at 13328 Granite Creek Road, San Diego, CA 92128. (858) 513-9293

Robert P. Ocker is a middle-school guidance counselor in Mondovi, Wisconsin. Through drama he helps students focus on problem solving, conflict resolution, student responsibility, and character education. Contact him at 7717 – 35th Ave., Knolsha, WI 53142

Cathy Patterson lives in Vancouver, British Columbia, Canada. She is a special education teacher working with students with severe behavior disorders. She helps school professionals and families collaborate to meet the needs of this special population.

Bibliography

Breggin, Peter R. (2002), *the Ritalin Fact Book*. Cambridge, MA.: Perseus Books Group.

Breggin, Peter R. (2001), *Talking Back to Ritalin*. Cambridge, MA.: Perseus Books Group.

Carroll, Lee and Tober, Jan. (2001), *An Indigo Celebration*. Carlsbad, CA: Hay House.

Carroll, Lee and Tober, Jan. (2001), *The Care and Feeding of Indigo Children*. Carlsbad, CA: Hay House.

Carroll, Lee and Tober, Jan. (1999), *The Indigo Children*. Carlsbad, CA: Hay House.

Tappe, Nancy. (1982), *Understanding Your Life Through Color*. Carlsbad, CA: Starling Publishers.

Notes

Notes

Notes

Notes